Translation and the Accommodation of Diversity

Jean Peeters / Jandhyala Prabhakara Rao (eds.)

Translation and the Accommodation of Diversity

Indian and non-Indian Perspectives

Bibliographic Information published by the Deutsche Nationalbibliothek
The Deutsche Nationalbibliothek lists this publication in the Deutsche Nationalbibliografie; detailed bibliographic data is available in the internet at http://dnb.d-nb.de.

The book was published with the support
of research laboratories HCTI,
Université de Bretagne-Sud and PREFICS,
Université de Bretagne-Sud
and Université de Rennes 2, France

Library of Congress Cataloging-in-Publication Data

Translation and the accommodation of diversity : Indian and non-Indian perspectives / Jean Peeters, Jandhyala Prabhakara Rao (eds.).
   pages cm
   ISBN 978-3-631-62651-1
   1. Translating and interpreting. 2. Multilingualism. 3. Sociolinguistics. I. Peeters, Jean, 1962- editor of compilation. II. Prabhakara Rao, Jandhyala, 1959- editor of compilation.
   P306.T695 2013
   418'.02—dc23
                                                              2013022663

ISBN 978-3-631-62651-1
© Peter Lang GmbH
Internationaler Verlag der Wissenschaften
Frankfurt am Main 2013
All rights reserved.
PL Academic Research is an Imprint of Peter Lang GmbH.

Peter Lang – Frankfurt am Main · Bern · Bruxelles · New York · Oxford · Warszawa · Wien

All parts of this publication are protected by copyright. Any utilisation outside the strict limits of the copyright law, without the permission of the publisher, is forbidden and liable to prosecution. This applies in particular to reproductions, translations, microfilming, and storage and processing in electronic retrieval systems.

www.peterlang.de

Introduction

Between 22-24 November, 2010, Université de Bretagne-Sud, France and University of Hyderabad, India, hosted an international conference on Translation and the Accommodation of Diversity: Indian and non-Indian Perspectives. This conference is a follow-up to the conference held at University of Hyderabad, India between 10 and 12 February 2010 and whose title was "Socio-Cultural Approaches to Translation: Indian and European Perspectives".

In line with the idea that translation is rooted in diversity and that its nature resides in accommodating differences of all sorts: lexical, textual, macrotextual, intertextual, individual, social, cultural, political, etc., the aim of the conference was to be a forum for discussion from perspectives anchored in different cultures and backgrounds. Although English is one of the languages of India, it reflects modes of thinking and daily experiences that can be very different from the West, where English is also one of many languages. Likewise, cultures in the West are not monolithic, in the same way that they can be very diverse in India too. So, translation becomes a balancing act between and within multilingualism and cultural diversity

This collection of papers, which deals with literature, poetry, hospital situations, minority languages, proverbs and so on, gives a good picture of how differences are accommodated in translation across languages but also across cultures. They form a good starting point for comparison between translation practices and translation approaches. They reveal how Indian and Western scholars perceive translation.

Jean Peeters and J. Prabhakara Rao

Table of Contents

Introduction 5

Blending Teaching with Research: English Translations of Pushkin's Eugene Onegin
Anna Ponomareva 9

Diversity Management for Poetry Translation at the Semantic and Formal Levels: "Psalm" by Lucian Blaga
Carmen-Ecaterina Aştirbei 25

Translation from Gallo to French in Brittany's Hospitals: Views about Methodology and Epistemology
Clément Ferré 37

Role and Value of Professional Translation in the European Union: A few leads on different scales
David Ar Rouz 53

Dissémination et triangle culturel: réalités orientales dans deux romans « algériens » contemporains de langue française
Mirela Kumbaro-Furxhi and Yves Gambier 73

Translation and the Dialectic of Continental Crossroads: A Case Study of Assam
Manjeet Baruah 87

Translating Culture Through Religion The works of women *Bhakta* saints
Meeta Narain 101

Translating Indian Language Proverbs: What do they Contribute to Translation Theory?
Panchanan Mohanty 111

TraduXio: A Collaborative Platform for Multilingual Translation
Philippe Lacour, Any Freitas, Aurélien Bénel, Diana Zambon and Franck Eyrau 121

Accommodation In Translation: An Indian Perspective
J. Prabhakara Rao and Jean Peeters 131

Multilingual Technical Translation –
A Case of Intercultural Communication
Sumedha Desai 135

Transelating Woman: Feminist Translation in Nicole Brossard
Sushma V. Murthy 145

Blending Teaching with Research: English Translations of Pushkin's Eugene Onegin

Anna Ponomareva

1. Introductory Remarks: Brahma and Vishnu

Any current person specification for a Lecturer in Translation looks more like the description of the Hindu Trinity – Brahma, Vishnu and Shiva – rather than a human being. In the symbolism of Hindu beliefs, Brahma is the creator, Vishnu is the preserver and Shiva is the destroyer. In the re-incarnation of Brahma, the Lecturer in Translation is responsible for the creative process or, using academic terminology, for research. Vishnu's role demands from the profession the preservation of divine or scholarly ideas, and parallels can be easily drawn with teaching responsibilities. The Lecturer turns into Shiva, the destroyer, when he or she is doing the job of Interpreter or Translator. This re-incarnation dictates its own rules and often the provision of Translation Services to customers in everyday life contradicts all theories of Translation.

The focus of this article is only two re-incarnations, Brahma and Vishnu, out of the listed three for a Lecturer in Translation. It will be shown how the demands of the profession push these two Indian gods to live in peace and harmony with each other. In other words, it will be demonstrated how one's research might be used in one's teaching. This approach, blending teaching with research, provides opportunities to students to enhance their experiences in a lecture hall and to deepen their understanding of new material because they feel invited to participate in their lecturer's creative activities. The article highlights some themes in the author's ongoing research in Intercultural Communication which is based on English translations of Pushkin's *Eugene Onegin*. It will be also argued that numerous translations of *Onegin* might be used as a companion to Pym's *Exploring Translation Theories* (2009) because they provide a unique material to illustrate various theoretical points of Pym's book.

2. Eugene Onegin in English as a companion to Pym's textbook

In every culture, there is a piece of literature, a novel, a poem or a play, which gets the attention and captures the imagination of the rest of the world, and has been translated into many foreign languages. Moreover, the chosen piece might be re-translated many times into one language. *The Thousand and One Nights* or *The Arabian Nights* as well as Pushkin's *Eugene Onegin* are just two examples of the same phenomenon. According to the bibliography of English translations of *Eugene Onegin* compiled and maintained by the York Bibliographic Society[1], at the moment there are at least twenty-four full verse translations of *Onegin* into English (without counting revised editions of the same translation). As many as eight translations appeared in the first decade of the 21st century. Hofstadter (1999), one of the translators of the Pushkin's novel, anticipating many readers' question, why people re-translate, addresses this issue in introduction to his *Onegin*:

> Did people stop climbing Everest when Hilary and Tenzing had climbed it? Does a good pianist stop playing a work simply because great recordings of it already exist? Of course not. People are driven to do their own thing precisely because of the wonderful accomplishments of others. (1999: xxix)

It appears to be admiration for the chosen subject and readiness to face the challenge are driving forces of re-translation. Numerous re-translations are not only evidence of the labour of love but they are ambitious projects too. What is more important for this research is that they are a unique teaching material.

The English translations of *Onegin* are written over the period of time which is nearly one hundred and thirty years, from 1881 to 2009. The impressive time scale of the work is in itself a guarantee of numerous variations in the interpretation of the original. It is easier to make references to one particular literary source and use its multiple metamorphoses as illustrations of translation theories. Counterarguments might be used against this claim by pointing to the emergence of Translation as an academic subject from other disciplines in the middle of the 20th century. It should not be taken seriously, because the non-existence of academic status does not stop people from doing translations, thinking and arguing about them.

Pym (2009) defines seven paradigms in translation theories. They are not bound to specific time; they might co-exist in particular periods. Each paradigm is the pool of ideas associated with one particular understanding of translation. He names the paradigms using key words which stand for their main concepts. They are:

- Natural equivalence
- Directional equivalence
- Purposes
- Descriptive
- Uncertainty

---

1 For more information see http://www-users.york.ac.uk/~pml1/onegin/.

- Localisation
- Cultural Translation.

Complementary to the publication of his book *Exploring Translation Theories* Pym presented a cycle of lectures at the Rovira i Virgili University in Tarragona, Spain, which highlights and clarifies its main concepts.[2] Explaining the concept of equivalence, Pym uses an unusual but explicit example from everyday life. He describes one's approach as unrealistic if this person tries to obtain an equivalent amount of gold for American dollar banknotes because there is a sign on the banknotes about its exchange into gold and rates. In this way, Pym argues that equivalence is theoretically possible but practically impossible.

The same applies to translation. Conceptually, various equivalence models in translation theories, natural, directional, aimed at purposes and norms, sooner or later provoke a different, in some cases, even directly opposite reaction. In the paradigm "Uncertainty", it appears that equivalence empties a space for deconstruction and transformation and points to the omnipotent indeterminacy of translation. Ideas which underpin the concept are transparent: translators are simply uncertain about the meaning of what they translate. This applies to multifaceted words, idioms and word plays. Consequently the problem of choice becomes an agenda for translators. Pym points to Venuti's contribution (1995) to translation theories mentioning his work on exploring the concepts of invisibility of translators, domesticating and foreignizing approaches and "remainder". All these concepts are complicated ones. Pym's and Venuti's trains of thoughts are better understood by students if they are illustrated by examples from translations. In addition to what Venuti offers as illustrations of his points, largely based on French and Italian literature, examples from English translations of Pushkin's *Eugene Onegin* are helpful too.

Onegin occupies a special place in Russian literature and culture. Previously citing the whole novel by heart was considered as evidence of one's nobility and intelligence. It is still part of the National Curriculum.

In this article, Onegin's letter to Tatyana is chosen as a sample. It is an important part of the novel in which Onegin's character shows a number of essential characteristics. The translations of the following scholars are used to exemplify the concepts listed above: Elton (1937), Arndt ([1963], 2002)[3], Elton revised by Briggs (1995), and Hofstadter (1999). The choice of these four translations is personal rather than based on any particular characteristics.

---

2   They are put online and are accessible at http://www.tinet.cat/~apym/publications/ETT/video_list.html
3   The first date indicates the year of first publication, the second date is the year of publication which is used in this work.

3. Invisibility

3.1 Concept

Invisibility is a relatively new term in Translation Studies. It is not defined by Shuttleworth and Cowie in their *Dictionary of Translation Studies* (1997). Venuti's famous book on Invisibility (1995) also avoids giving a proper definition for the term; instead he suggests its associative sequence by listing fluency, transparency and domestication as members. Venutu (1995: 8) also perceives the term politically and makes a link between the unrecognized authorship of the translator's work and the rights of translators as citizens in Britain and the US. The book ends with the expression of his strong belief in the power of translation that is able to make a difference. Venuti writes, "To recognize the translator's invisibility is at once to critique the current situation and to hope for a future more hospitable to the differences that the translator must negotiate." (1995: 313)

Terminological complexity of invisibility is obvious even from the above given details. Clarification is needed. A number of crucial points relevant to the term are going to be discussed using examples from the four chosen English translations of *Onegin*. Firstly, the focus will be on the physical appearance of translation publications. Secondly, the presence of translator's name on cover and title pages will be checked. The issues of self-publicity will be discussed later, when introductory chapters are analyzed. The investigation will continue focusing on the text of translations of Onegin's letter to Tatyana.

3.2 Do covers have translators' names?

Usually publishing houses are responsible for the covers of their editions. Their choice would be approved by the team of professionals who are involved in the edition. Without any doubt, translators do take part in choosing images for the covers of their work. Covers are important because they provide first-hand information on their book's content. In the case of translations, covers stress either the strangeness or similarity of content for readers.

Professor Simmons who wrote the review of the first four published translations in verse of *Eugene Onegin* into English, is pleased with the appearance of Elton's publication. According to Simmons, "Pushkin loved beautiful books, and he would have been delighted with the handsome edition that contains Professor Elton's translation." (1938: 204) It was published in 1937, the centennial of Pushkin's death. There are only 775 copies. One of them, copy number 197, is kept in the British Library. It looks impressive, a big volume of A4 size. It looks beautiful too. Its typography is free from any eccentricity: each page is a clear, well-balanced printed set in Monotype Walbaum type which came to England from Germany in 1925 where it was previously used to publish classical texts. The book has illustrations by M.V. Dobuzhinsky, but there is none on its front cover. It is a typically academic edition.

The design of three other translations is directed to a wider readership. Their size is common for a reading book. They have images on their covers to attract the diversity of readers. A painting, Michael's Castle, by A.P. Bogolyubov is on Arndt's work.[4] It gives an idea of the country of the novel and the architecture of the castle, built in 1797-1801, suggests the time. Briggs' revision of Elton's translation has a portrait. It is Man Reading by Lamplight by George Friedrich Kersting (1785-1847), a German painter. The way in which Kersting positions his character implies that the man is not in the natural world, but within himself, in his imagination. This suggests that the place is not important. The portrait being not culturally specific is bounded, however, by time. The man is in the nineteenth century costume. Hofstadter's work has a drawing of the Peter and Paul Fortress which symbolizes St Petersburg and the power of the Russian Tsars. As an embodiment of strong military and political control, the fortress was the place where a number of senior officers-rebels were kept after the Decembrist uprising in 1825. In this drawing the place and time of the novel are essentially represented.

If the back covers of Elton's and Briggs/Elton's work have information about the novel, Hofstadter's translation has a photo of the translator sitting in his cabinet under the portrait of Pushkin on the wall. There is also information on the previous Hofstadter's publications next to the photo.

The cover of Hofstadter's work looks unusual in the bookshops of English-speaking countries. First of all, it provides more information on the translator rather than on the author of the original. It is also requires a knowledge of Russian history in order to be understood in full. Under the guidance of Hofstadter, it sends its prospective readers to a strange and foreign land.

Translators' names are mentioned on title pages of their work but they are introduced differently. The work of Elton, Briggs/Elton and Arndt are translations. Hofstadter's work is a novel versification. Arndt's and Hofstadter's names are appeared on the covers of their work.

Cover design, information presented there as well as on the front pages direct one's attention immediately to Hofstadter's visibility. To him, making himself visible helps Pushkin's Onegin to be more accessible to an English speaking audience. He believes if the translator is not obliged to cover his or her presence in

---

[4] Here is a description of the second revised edition that Arndt prepared in 1981. The copy I used is a reprint of this edition published by Ardis Publishers in 2002. The first edition does not look a lot different, there is just another picture on the front cover. The Ardis publication is used as an example because it was easier accessible.

the translated text, equivalence is not an issue. To him, liberation from the original provides opportunities for the translator to communicate openly with readers.

3.3 Translator's Preface: a place for self-publicity?

Each chosen translation has an introduction or preface or both, written by the translators themselves. Again differences here are significant. Elton's introduction has twelve pages, only three out of these twelve pages are devoted to explaining the peculiarities of his translation. By pointing to the similarities and differences in English and Russian, rhymes and the linear character of Pushkin's verse, Elton assumes that there are opportunities to translate between these two languages and to produce "an original poem in English". This argument shows that Elton's translation strategy might be domestication and equivalence is considered.

Briggs edits Elton's translation in preparing a new edition of *Onegin* for Everyman Publishers. It has the introduction of eleven pages, two out of these eleven are relevant to translation issues. It has also further explanatory material, Note on the Text, which is only three pages long. Briggs, like Elton, starts with pointing to similarities between English and Russian but concludes that these advantages "will soon dissolve". The focus of his editing is to remove Elton's archaisms and to correct inaccuracies.

Arndt's work has a two-page preface with some commentaries on translation and a nine-page introduction. His major concerns are the acoustic qualities of his translation. In his text, in order to encourage his readers to pronounce correctly Russian names Arndt puts stresses on them. He also tries to sharpen his lines, so "the iambic meter should be the reader's guide." The way in which Arndt deals with Russian names suggests an element of foreignizing strategy in his translation. He has retained the sparkle of the original which can be also understood as an attempt to maintain the metric gadgetry.

All three scholars provide extremely limited or no information about themselves and how they did their translation. They share the concept of the invisibility of translators.

Reading a more than thirty-page long preface by Hofstadter, one is able to understand that invisibility is not an issue for this translator. In his preface, Hofstadter invites his readers to go along the stages of his work and to be aware of their turns and twists. Some critics might understand this approach as a self-publicity exercise. For example, according to McMillin, Hofstadter's Translator's Preface is "garrulous", "a blow-by-blow account of how he learned (some) Russian for the purpose of popularizing Pushkin's novel in verse" (2001: 313). Others might disagree with this criticism. Hofstadter is famous enough; he does not need publicity. His intention is different, to invite readers to his theatre of mind and to see, as if from inside his brain, what is going on there. Firstly, he is a cognitive scientist, and secondly, he is a translator. To any scholar of Translation, Hofstadter's preface is a unique material which highlights the insights of one's thinking and the translation process.

4. Domesticating or Foreignizing

Venuti argues, "We can more fully understand the translators' different motives and practices by considering their translations in the context of their other work, their lives, and their different historical moments." (1995: 93) The case of *Onegin* in English proves this point. In the next part of my article, it will be highlighted how the personalities of translators impact their work and choice of strategies.

4.1 Elton: part of the noble heritage of English literature

Oliver Elton (1861-1945), an English literary scholar and the author of *A Survey of English Literature (1730-1880)*, was also a translator. He translated from Icelandic and Russian. Elton's translation of *Eugene Onegin* was among three other verse translations into English which appeared in 1937 to commemorate the centenary of Pushkin's death. Elton's work is read as good poetry in English. It is written in archaic English, the language which was used not in the 19the century but before that. It is unlikely that Elton's intention was to send his readers to another epoch to foreignize his translation of *Onegin* as one might suggest after reading Venuti's chapter on Margin where Ezra Pound's experiments, his particularly archaic English, in using foreignizing translation are explained. One of them is presented in Mayor's words, in his analysis of Pound's translation of Guido Cavalcanti, a Florentine poet of the 13th century:

> The quaint language is not a pastiche of pre-Shakespearen sonnets, or an attempt to make Cavalcanti talk Elizabethan the way Andrew Lang made Homer try to talk King James. Ezra Pound is matching Cavalcanti's early freshness with a color lifted from the early freshness of English poetry. (Cited after Venuti 1995: 202 of Mayor (1932))

By using archaic English Elton feels at home and helps his readers to feel comfortable too. It is his understanding of poetic canons. It was the poetry taught at school at that time. Evidence can be easily found Elton's other work. In his *Survey of English Literature 1730-1880* he makes a clear comment on the value of the work of the past masters:

The reviewer of the romantic period must begin by calling for justice to the age of reason; he must, for his own sake, be fair to the first three quarters of the eighteenth century. We have not the privilege of Blake and Wordsworth and Keats, who were rebels and liberators, and whose business it was to be ungrateful. We are likely to think too little rather than too much of the writers who are termed classical, and who have long ceased to be dangerous. (Elton, 1920: 42)

Elton's translation of *Onegin* is an example of keeping "classical literature firmly in mind" (1920: 43). Elton domesticates his translation of Pushkin's 19th century novel in verse using the 18th century English poetic language. The same argument is echoed in Simmons words: "... I regard Professor Elton's translation as a genuine and lasting addition to the series of great translations which have become part of the noble heritage of English literature." (1938: 207)

4.2 Elton/Briggs: an attempt to look younger in your 60s

Anthony Briggs, a Russian scholar and translator of Tolstoi and Pushkin, revised Elton's *Onegin* in 1995. To some extent, it is a strange situation. Life, however, provides simple explanations. As a consultant editor at that time, in charge of Russian literature, for Everyman Paperback he recommended Pushkin's novel for publication, but did not have enough time to produce his own version and chose Elton's translation as it did not have copyrights. A new version is a hybrid text, a work of two translation scholars who belong to different times and use various types of English.

Briggs randomly keeps some of Elton's archaic expressions and also changes a number of them using a modern version of English. Below there are just few examples:

Elton (1937)	Elton/Briggs (1995)
(p. 231)'By chance, I met you once of old;	(p. 193) 'We once met; it was accidental.
(p. 231) Unbound, – myself from all estranging, I thought (my God! How much amiss, At what a cost!) that I was bliss For rest and freedom well exchanging.	(p. 194) An outcast, free from all restriction, I thought in freedom to possess A substitute for happiness. What a mistake! What an infliction!...
(p. 232) And yet, to shield each glance and phrase With coldness and dissimulation; To join in quite conversation, And look – on you – with cheerful gaze!...	(p. 195) Meanwhile I must appear phlegmatic, My tongue and eyes well fortified. My speech is calm, but, at your side, Glancing at you, I feel ecstatic.
(p. 232) 'So be it; I am weak, am quitting My inward struggle; all I see, It settled; do you will with me, And to my fate I am submitting.'	(p. 195) 'So be it. I decline at last To fight myself; my strength is slender. I'm in your hands; the die is cast. To destiny I now surrender.'

"Accidental", "an outcast", "phlegmatic", "ecstatic" and especially "the die is cast" are tags of the end of the 20th century English. "The die is cast" is what Julian Caesar said in Latin when he with his army crossed the river Rubicon. The expression, however, started to be widely used after the Deep Space Nine episode of *The Star Trek,* an American science fiction TV programme.

Behind Briggs' editing is his intention to rejuvenate the nearly 60-year-old Elton text and make it accessible to wider audiences; not only to an educated elite which is used to reading and memorising classic poetry at school but also to the contemporary young generation.

In my correspondence with Briggs, he mentioned that he is going to produce his own translation of *Eugene Onegin* in the near future. According to Briggs, translators' intention to retranslate is based on two reasons. The first reason is similar to Hofstadter's argument mentioned before. The second reason is "the certainty that they can do better than those who went before. ... they all think they can make an improvement."[5] This shows that Briggs himself understands that there is room for improvement in his revision of Elton's translation. It is too early to comment on a strategy he is going to use in his work. His Note on the Text, however, suggests that domesticating approach might be an option. Explaining his replacement of feminine rhymes based on particles (in the given above example, they are "quitting/submitting"), Briggs stands for a "more natural speech pattern" (1995: xxviii). Briggs also provides an interesting rational to change the spelling of Onegin's first name, from Eugene to Yevgeny, by arguing that Eugene "sounds slightly strange, rather unEglish. It is uncommon on mainland Britain; most Eugenes are Irish or American. By contrast, 'Yevgeny' sounds middle-of-the road, thoroughly normal and Russian to a native speaker of that language." (Briigs/Elton, 1995: xxviii) Briggs, however, attacks not so much Elton – he uses Evgeny as the first name for the main character – but other translators' work. Here nothing is said about a possible translation strategy but there is a hint, "middle-of-the road", which might be utilized later in his translation of *Eugene Onegin.*

Not only the story with the first name of the main Pushkin's character but also criticism of Johnston's translation, in which lines start not necessarily with capital letters as in the original, point to equivalence as Brigg's aim. It shows the uncertainty that Briggs faces in choosing his translation strategy. Even the small element of foreignizing, the spelling of Onegin's first name, demands to be balanced with a domesticating thinking pattern.

---

5   I extremely grateful to Professor Briggs for his intention to help me; he spend his valuable time in correspondence with me. Professor Briggs kindly answered my questions in his e-mail of 18 November 2010.

"Middle-of-the-road" might be Briggs' strategy too, in his editing Elton's work. It will be interesting to see his own translation of *Onegin* soon.

4.3 Arndt: the Anglicization of Onegin in a truly German way

Walter Arndt's translation was published in 1963. It was honoured by that year's Bollingen Prize for poetry translation. A native speaker of German, a Professor of Russian and the translator of Goethe and Raine Maria Rilke became the rival to Nabokov by publishing his translation first. In the foreword to his literal translation Nabokov argues:

> I have been always amused by the stereotyped compliment that a reviewer pays the author of a "new translation". He says: "It reads smoothly." In other words, the hack who has never read the original, and does not know its language, praises an imitation as readable because easy platitudes have replaced in it the intricacies of which he is unaware. "Readable", indeed! A schoolboy's boner mocks the ancient masterpiece less than does its commercial poetization, and it is when the translator sets out to render the "spirit", and not the more sense of the text, that he begins to traduce his author. (1964: ix)

Arndt's name is not mentioned in the quote above but can be easily read between the lines. In other places, Nabokov is happy to attack everything that Arndt, to a large extent, managed to maintain from the Pushkin text, rhyme, rhythm and literary grace. Nabokov's descriptive words and metaphors related to Arndt's work sometimes go beyond the limits of any vocabulary acceptable in scholarly criticism.

Arndt's translation is an acoustic one. When it is read aloud it gives a pleasure to hear the melody of Pushkin's iambic tetrameter in English. Edmund Wilson, an American writer and literary and social critic, praises his translation highly. In making comparisons between Arndt's and Nabokov's work in his review, *The Strange Case of Pushkin and Nabokov,* Wilson (1965) describes Arndt's work as "the tour de force of translating", "a heroic effort". He also argues the presence of non-English elements in both translations: "If it is a question of picking on Germanisms in Arndt, it is not difficult to find Russianisms in Nabokov". Hofstadter admires Arndt's work, too, but underlines his Anglicization of *Onegin.* (1999: xxiii)

There were no examples given of any Germanisms and Anglicization in Arndt's work. To me, his translation is evidence of German perfectionism expressed in English.[6] Arndt domesticates the Pushkin text in the environment of poetic English but he uses a foreignizing strategy in maintaining the delightful sounds of Pushkin poetry. For instance, the omnipotent accuracy of rhythmic

---

6 To check the quality of Arndt's English my colleagues at Imperial College London, the native speakers of English and scholars of German, were asked.

mosaics is responsible for his acoustic versatility. Hofstadter defines it as "symmetric translation". He argues that Arndt imitates the Pushkin gesture of starting and ending his entire work with the same word, Pushkin's "my" transforms to Arndt's "now" (1999: xxiii). To him, this is evidence of Arndt's astuteness.

There more examples of this type in the text. Just looking at the first few lines of Onegin's letter to Tatyana one is able to see a number of Arndt's symmetric ornamental patterns.

	Pushkin	Arndt
1	Предвижу всё: вас оскорбит	I doubt not: I shall give offense
2	Печальной тайны объясненье.	By baring secrets dark and painful;
3	Какое горькое презренье	What glances bitterly disdainful
4	Ваш гордый взгляд изобразит!	Your haughty eye will now dispense!
5	Чего хочу? С какою целью	What do I seek? For what employment
6	Открою душу вам свою?	Do I expose my soul to you?
7	Какому злобному веселью,	And how much mischievous enjoyment,
8	Быть может, повод подаю!	It may be, give occasion to?

Pushkin's verbs at the ending of line 1 and 4 are matched by Arndt's *offense/defense* that are either part of the construction which specify an action (to give offense = to offend) or a verb (to dispense). The Russian stressed syllable '*um*' is changed into the English '*ens*'. Nouns, the endings of line 2 and 3 of the original, are transformed by Arndt into two rhythmic adjectives, *painful/disdainful*. In this way, the unstressed 'е' becomes the unstressed 'ful'. Pushkin's *целью/веселью* is symmetrical to *employment/enjoyment* in the translation of lines 5 and 7: the unstressed 'ю' corresponds to the unstressed 'ment'. In the original, the endings represented by different grammatical categories in lines 6 and 8, one is a possessive pronoun *свою*, another is *подаю*, a verb in the present tense first-person singular form. Arndt matches them with a pronoun '*you*' and a verb with a preposition '*give to*'. It is even possible to hear how Pushkin's 'ю' is echoed in Arndt's 'you/to'. This symmetry is unlikely to be deliberate; to me, it is evidence of Arndt's paramount attention to detail or technical accuracy which is the culturally specific characteristic of German people.

Arndt himself argues the existence and necessity of linguistic patters in *Traduttori, Traditori?* His article on the prosody of English highlights the following elements:

> English resources of rhyme and rhythm within the given range of lexical elements may accommodate us – even into half the kingdom – by a constellation of happy coincidence and restless ingenuity; and if we then make the unit of translation large enough, we may hope, through a kind of mosaic technique, to achieve a similarly harmonious pattern of linguistic building stones, associative clays, and rhythmic pattern. (1965: 4)

The acoustic pleasure of Arndt's work is due to his use of domesticating strategy but the result is prolific because his foreignizing efforts make possible the fulfillment of Arndt's Anglicization plan for *Onegin*.

4.4 Hofstadter: 20th century jazzy versification of the 19th century masterpiece

The growing of foreignizing elements in translation strategy continues in other English *Onegins*. Hofstadter's novel versification is its vivid example. The unusual design of his book cover and the presence of his personality in introductory chapters have been previously mentioned. Now is the time to look at his translation.

Hofstadter is fond of Falen's translation of *Eugene Onegin* (1990). He makes this clear in his introduction. His intention to produce another translation of the Pushkin novel seems illogical as, in his opinion, Falen's work is "truly à la Pushkin". Remembering, however, Briggs' explanations why translators are happy to re-translate, it becomes clear that there is room for improvement in any translation, even in Falen's work. Hofstadter adds to the existing collection of English *Onegin*s a playful spirit correctly spotting it in Pushkin's work. Sometimes he goes too far. Hofstadter, however, anticipates a possible criticism and names his work a versification, not a translation. It is a truly creative piece of writing. Moreover, according to Adrian Wanner (2000), a review of Hofstadter's *Onegin,* " Hofstadter ...challenges the stale claim of equivalence to a fetishized original text." (2000: 84)

His versification of the novel is read as a translation and introduces a number of peculiar Russian features to readers using the medium of Englishes. It is full of colloquialisms, contemporary expressions as well as formal ones. His intention to signify the foreignness of the foreign text is similar to Pound's and Blackburn's experiments in translation described by Venuti (1995) in his chapter Margin. Sharing similar techniques with them Hofstadter deviates from the literary canons in English and violates the translated text. He does so in order to move his readers closer to the original.

5. Reminder

Hofstadter's work is a good illustration of what a reminder is. According to Jean-Jacques Lecercle (1990) is it an effect of homophonic translation, a release of multiple meanings specific to English, "what exceeds transparent uses of language geared to communication and reference and may in fact impede them, with varying degrees of violence." (Cited after Venuti 1995: 216) In Onegin's letter to Tatyana, it is possible to find at least two reminders, 'helter-skelter' and 'Les jeux sont faits'.

Helter-skelter might be referring to a song from the White Album by the Beatles (1968) and to a spiral slide, a ride in an amusement park. It is used by Hofstadter to translate *наудачу*. Nabokov believes that it has an equivalent in English – 'at random'. The expression appears when Pushkin's Onegin tries to describe his hectic movements one day, to try to see Tatyana quite by chance; as he is waiting for her reply and cannot visit her without an invitation. Describing Onegin's movements as helter-skelter Hofstadter argues the elements of purposeless and the lack of planning in his activities. He uses 'to run', a complete opposite to Pushkin's description, *тащиться* (to go slowly), not only due to a collocation problem (one is not able to go slowly and helter-skelter at the same time), but also to emphasise that running around helter-skelter is pointless, boring and painful. This is exactly what Onegin means by describing his useless days in the letter to Tatyana. In tandem with the previous line, "But I'm deprived of this; for you," the following line "I run around all helter-skelter;" is an example where the colloquial expression adds extra meaning and also signals to problems in understanding the original. The similar technique is highlighted by Venuti when he writes about Blackburn:

> Yet Blackburn's prosodic experiments give all this an anti-individualistic edge by pushing the verse towards greater heterogeneity, using rhythm, punctuation, typography to foreground the textuality and erode the coherence of the speaking voice, now a site of diverse lexicons, cultural codes, social affiliations, whose very juxtaposition invites a mutual questioning. (1995: 263)

Another reminder is 'Les jeux sont faits' that is used for *Всё решено* ('All is decided' by Nabokov). The French instead of English expression highlights the specific feature of Onegin's behaviour and thinking. Like Pushkin, Onegin is a gambler. To him, life is a game. Sending his love letter to Tatyana Onegin behaves as if he risks all his money in gambling in a casino. In this case, Hofstadter's intention of foreignizing Pushkin's phrase makes its meaning more visual and realistic. By deviating from the text Hofstadter comes closer to Pushkin's ideas.

Meanwhile, one can easily agree with Wanner (2000: 84) that, in spite of all Hofstadter's "jazzy burlesque" attempts, it is a "rewarding experience". Arnold McMillin (2001) confirms that reading Hofstadter's versification gives him "pleasure as well as aggravation". He also hopes that it might attract a younger audience. My students of Russian, intelligent young people from Imperial College, have been encouraged to read the four chosen translations and to express their preferences. According to their responses, the majority of students enjoy reading Hofstadter's *Onegin*. This shows that Hofstadter's work serves its purpose.

6. Concluding remarks

Concluding my article it is appropriate to mention that my research on the translation strategies, domesticating and foreignizing, is far from being completed. A lot of hypotheses should be checked and a lot of more, hopefully, will come. At this stage, what it is absolutely clear is that English *Onegin*s can provide stimulating material for a translation course. The translating strategies, domesticating and foreignizing, can be illustrated by the rich and powerful examples from a number of translations. These strategies do not exclude each other, are not necessarily historically bound. They simply signal the translator's intention either to be invisible and produce a fluent text or to be visible and violate the original in order to enhance readers' experience of the foreign text.

References

Arndt, Walter. "Traduttori, Traditori?" *South Atlantic Bulletin* Vol. 29, No. 3 (May, 1964): 1-5.
Elton, Oliver. 1920. *A Survey of English Literature 1730-1880.* Vol 1. New York: The Macmillan Company. Available online http://www.onread.com/reader/1321404 Accessed 13 February 2011.)
Falen, James. 1995. *Eugene Onegin.* Oxford, New York: Oxford University Press.
Lecercle, J.-J. 1990. *The Violence of Language.* London and New York: Routledge.
Mayor, A.H. "Cavalcanti and Pound", *Hound and Horn* Vol. 5, No. 3 (April-June, 1932): 468-71.
McMillin, Arnold. "Eugene Onegin: A Novel in Verse. A Novel Versification by Alexander Sergeevich Pushkin", *The Slavonic and East European Review* Vol. 79, No. 2 (April, 2001): 313-315.
Pushkin, Aleksandr. 1978. Polnoe sobranie sochinenii v desyati tomakh. Tom V. Evgenii Onegin.
Dramaticheskie proizvedeniya. Leningrad: Izdatel'stvo "Nauka".
– *Evgeny Onegin.* Translated by Oliver Elton. 1937. London: The Pushkin Press.
– *Eugene Onegin.* Translated by James Falen. 1990. Carbondale, Illinois: Southern Illinois University Press.
– *Eugene Onegin: A Novel in Verse.* Translated by Vladimir Nabokov. 1964. London: Routledge & Kegan Paul.

- *Eugene Onegin.* Translated by Charles Johnston. 1977. London: Penguin Books.
- *Yevgeny Onegin.* Translated by Oliver Elton [1937]; edited and revised by A.D.P. Briggs. 1995. London, Vermont: Everyman.
- *Eugene Onegin. A Novel Versification* by Douglas Hofstadter. 1999. New York: Basic Books.
- *Eugene Onegin.* Translated by Walter Arndt. 2002. Woodstock & New York: Ardis Publishers.

Pym, Anthony. 2009. *Exploring Translation Theories.* London: Routledge.

Shuttleworth, Mark & Cowie, Moira. 1997. *Dictionary of translation studies.* Manchester: St. Jerome.

Simmons, Ernest. "English Translations of Eugene Onegin", *The Slavonic and East European Review* Vol. 17, No 49 (Jul., 1938): 198-208.

Venuti, Lawrence. 1995. The Translator's Invisibility: A history of translation. London and New York: Routledge.

Wanner, Adrian. "Eugene Onegin. A Novel in Verse by Alexander Sergeevich Pushkin by Douglas Hofstadter", *Comparative Literature Studies* Vol. 37, No. 1 (2000): 83-86.

Wilson, Edmund. "The Strange Case of Pushkin and Nabokov", *The New York Review of Books* Vol. 4, No 12 (July, 1965). Available online: http://www.nybooks.com/articles/12829 Accessed 15 February 2011.

Diversity Management for Poetry Translation at the Semantic and Formal Levels: "Psalm" by Lucian Blaga[1]

Carmen-Ecaterina Aştirbei

1. Diversity of Translation Studies approaches. The ancient "dispute" between form and content

Translating is a complex activity implying a multiplicity of levels: lexical, textual, macrotextual, intertextual, individual, social, cultural and even political. This complexity constitutes the diversity itself of translation. Especially in case of poetry, the semantic and formal elements, but also the possible cultural implicatures form its specificity. The translator may see in the signifier-signified dichotomy of the poetic text an insuperable difficulty or, on the contrary, he/she may choose to take advantages from this diversity and to create new linguistic figures in the source language. This diversity of the formal and semantic levels gives the translator the possibility to choose original techniques and to create, practically, a "second poetry" in the target language.

The debate concerning the permanence of the same signified during the transport of meaning from the source language to the target language is already famous in the field of Translation Studies. Our question is if it's better to preserve the message or if the form is more important in case of poetry translation. Torn between form and meaning and overwhelmed by "the imposture of sign" (Meschonnic, 1972: 50), the translator must take important decisions and adopt methods and strategies in order to express in the target language the richness of the original poem.

One may notice that, beside the diversity of levels, we also find a diversity of approaches concerning translation itself. From this point of view, there is a fundamental dichotomy in the field of Translations Studies between the source text and the translated one, which is considered different from the original. Hence, not only the secondary place of any translation in the target language, but also the never-ending questions concerning the necessity to adequately reproduce in

---

[1] The documentation and reseacrh for this work were supported by the European Social Fund in Romania, under the responsibility of the Managing Authority for the Sectorial Operational Program for Human Resources Development 2007-2013 [grant POSDRU/88/1.5/S/47646].

the target language the semantic and formal aspects of the linguistic sign from the source language, in other words, questions concerning the expression of diversity. Henri Meschonnic makes a capital distinction between the original text and the translation, which is seen as a text in itself:

> Si la traduction d'un texte est structurée-reçue comme un texte, elle fonctionne comme texte, elle est l'écriture d'une lecture-écriture, aventure historique d'un sujet. Elle n'est pas transparence par rapport à l'original. (1972: 50)[2]

Therefore, practical experience minimized the role of translation compared to the source text, thus giving priority to the writing in relation with the translation. Meschonnic continues: "Même la théorie linguistique de la traduction, par son dualisme, ne théorise pas le même travail sur la langue, pour le texte et pour la traduction." (1972: 51)[3]

Poetry, the one that drives us to "the disturbance of all senses", as Rimbaud claimed, is, in fact, signified encoded in a perfect shape which is, in itself, meaningful. That's why we consider that the formal level, the prosodic one, constitutes a second meaning, which one cannot ignore. The target language must dispose of all its "secret forces" in order to produce a comprehensible version which could come up to the value of the original text and thus, to deal in an effective manner with its diversity while translating.

In fact, even in case of poetry translation, the first function of language is to communicate the signified, beyond the form that the signified may achieve. Translation is one of the communication processes, because, in Jakobson's opinion:

> En traduisant d'une langue à l'autre, on remplace les messages des deux langues, non pas par des unités séparées d'un code, mais par des messages entiers d'une autre langue. Une telle traduction est une sorte de discours indirect: le traducteur confie et transmet le message reçu dans une autre langue. (1975: 65)[4]

The duality of poetry is given by the harmony between form and content which creates its diversity. The solution suggested by Jakobson in order to express the diversity characterizing the poetic text is the so-called "creative transposition":

---

2   "If the translation of a text is structured-received as a text, it does function as a text, it is writing of a reading-writing, historical adventure of a topic. It is not transparent compared to the original" (our translation).
3   "Even the linguistic theory of translation, by its dualism, does not theorize the same approach to language, for the text and for the translation" (our translation).
4   "While translating from one language to another, we replace the messages from the two languages, not with some units separated by a code, but with whole messages from another language. Such a translation is a kind of indirect discourse: the translator entrusts and transmits the message received in another language" (our translation).

> En poésie, les équations verbales sont promues au rang de principe constructif du texte. [...] La paronomase règne sur l'art poétique; que cette domination soit absolue ou limitée, la poésie, par définition, est intraduisible. Seule est possible la transposition créatrice. (2003: 86)[5]

Poetry, conglomerate of meaning and of "verbal equations", would become expression in itself of diversity. In other words, if diversity exists, there is also creativity of choice in translation.

Maurice Pergnier states that any translation approach is the result of an exegesis of a "privileged reader" ("lecteur privilégié") (1999: 161), or, as Umberto Eco calls him, "an ideal reader". As the original poem, by its diversity, is open to interpretation, translation becomes expression of its author's hermeneutics. Thus, poetry translation turns out to be possible and open to several possibilities. On the other hand, poetic language implies a referential dimension, but also a stylistic and aesthetic dimension, which requires from the translator a good control of diversity and, especially, *an effort to render the target text poetical*, as the source text is.

The translator's task does not consist in the strict reproduction of the message, despising the formal envelope. The translator is faced with the fugacity of poetry, which is considered a linguistic "deviation", as it breaks the rules of the common logics of language. If we do not take into consideration the diversity generated by the lyrical text, the conflict between signifier and signified may lead some scholars to postulate its untranslatability:

> Singulièrement quand il s'agit de traduction, la réflexion commence toujours par s'interroger sur la possibilité même de la pratique qu'elle prend pour objet, bien plus, la tendance lourdement prédominante est de conclure à l'impossibilité de traduire! C'est un paradoxe, bien étrange et semble-t-il tout à fait propre à la traduction. (Ladmiral, 1979: 85)[6]

And, referring to the dichotomy between the original text and the translated one, discussed by Meschonnic, one can consider that it constitutes an important obstacle for any poetry translation. In this sense, expressing the semantic and formal levels in the target language would be impossible:

> L'intraduisible comme texte est alors l'effet culturel résultant de ces raisons historiques. L'intraduisible est social et historique, non métaphysique (l'incommunicable, l'ineffable, le mystère, le génie). Tant que le moment de la traduction-texte n'est pas venu, l'effet translin-

---

5   "In poetry, verbal equations are promoted to the level of constructive principle of the text. [...] Paronomasia reigns over the poetic art; if this domination is or is not limited, poetry, by definition, is untranslatable. Creative transposition is the only possible way" (our translation).

6   "Especially in case of translation, any thought begins by questioning the very possibility of practice that it takes as an object; even more, the predominant tendency is to conclude that translation is impossible! It's a quite strange paradox, which seems to characterize translation in general" (our translation).

guistique est un effet de transcendance, et l'intraduisible passe pour une nature, un absolu. (Meschonnic, 1972: 51)[7]

The formal, semantic, social or historical untranslatability may be the direct effect of the contempt for the poetical text.

Contrary to the untranslatability theory, we postulate that the balance between form and content is not necessarily broken in translation if diversity is well dealt with. In fact, what does it mean to translate poetry? And what are the elements that appeal to the reader on the formal level? He is fascinated by "les mouvements et les arrêtes, le flux sonore et la rime, le centre et la distance entre les termes et l'image" (Kibédi-Varga, 1979: 270)[8]. Thus, it seems that translation is a double approach: one may speak about *the recreation of the iconic structure of the poem*, but also about *the recreation of the formal structure of the poem*, using the means of the target language. Because, in fact, and this is an important point of our analysis, the formal level constitutes a "second signified" during the translation process.

On one hand, there is diversity of form, and, on the other hand, diversity of content. Prosodic facts were criticized because of their necessary, but insufficient character: the translator cannot express them in the target language using the same strategies as in the source language; he/she should resort to the recreation of the formal poetical structure. Kibédi-Varga considers that the necessity of versification, doubled by its insufficiency, becomes a real touchstone for the translator:

> Ce qui caractérise les faits de versification bruts, c'est à la fois leur nécessité et leur insuffisance. Ils sont nécessaires parce qu'aucun poème ne saurait exister sans un certain nombre d'entre eux, mais ils sont insuffisants parce qu'à eux seuls, ils sont dépourvus de cette force de tension et de cohésion qui crée les rapports, les faits de poétique. On pourrait même soutenir que, paradoxalement, plus les faits de versification sont nécessaires, plus ils sont insuffisants. (1979: 44)[9]

---

7 "Untranslatability as a text is, therefore, the cultural effect resulting from these historical reasons. Untranslatability is social and historical; it does not have a metaphysical nature (as the inexpressible, the ineffable, the mystery, the genius). As the moment of the translation-text has not come yet, the translinguistic effect is *an effect of transcendence*, and untranslatability is considered a natural feature, an absolute one" (our translation).

8 "(…) the movements and the pauses, the sound flux and the rhyme, the center and the distance between terms and image" (our translation).

9 "The main feature of pure versification facts is, on one hand, their necessity and, on the other hand, their insufficiency. They are necessary because no poem could exist without some versification facts, but they are insufficient because, in themselves, they lack this tension and cohesion force which creates relations, poetical facts. One could even postulate that, paradoxically, the more necessary the versification facts are, the more insufficient they are." (our translation).

Nevertheless, we wonder why the versification elements, so important for the reception of a poem, always acquire a secondary place in case of a translation. Prosodic facts are meaningful in themselves, as in case of the sonnet or of the anagram. The role of the translator is to resort to techniques and strategies in order to create "the dynamic equivalence" (Nida). The translator should not betray the double content of the source text (on the semantic and formal level) and should satisfy, at the same time, the target audience; thus, he/she will take into account liberties and constraints in order to "match the morning words with the evening ones" (Berman, 1999: 83). This could be done by using those tricks that allow the translator to reveal to the reader of the target text the overwhelming complexity of the source language and source culture.

Beyond the distinction between form and content, poetry itself matters. We do neither strictly translate the phonology, nor the message as a separate component. It is true that this duality of the poem which comprises, on one hand, a prosodic and formal level, and, on the other hand, a semantic level, creates its unusual force. A translation which aims at breaking this harmony is doomed to failure. The poem requires from the reader some cognitive and emotive components; it unsettles the common logic; it captures the audience's attention sometimes to paroxysm. If we translate only the form, this "second signified", without paying much attention to the semantic content of the poem, the latter will be mutilated if deprived of its first meaning. In this context, our question is how to outdo this "imposture of sign" and how to treat its duality in translation in order to express its diversity in the target language? To illustrate this duality of the linguistic sign in translation, we propose the analysis of two translations into French of the poem "Psalm" written by the Romanian poet Lucian Blaga.

2. "Psalm" by Lucian Blaga – or how to deal with diversity at the semantic and formal levels

In order to support our idea, we chose the poem "Psalm" written by Lucian Blaga, and two translation variants in French. It constitutes a mystic confession which has as a starting point the quest for God. As far as the control of diversity is concerned, the translator will take into consideration first of all the formal level. The poem is structured in the form of a classical psalm, comprising four stanzas, which can be seen as four biblical "verses". But, compared to the "Psalms" of David from the Old Testament, this poem becomes, through its message, a sort of "antipsalm", an expression of the fear of nothingness. It is included in the volume "In the Great Passage", expression of the anxiety concerning the imminence of extinction and of the poet's silence faced with the mysteries in the world.

The translator will also notice, at the formal level, the structure of the "verses" expressing without doubt the poet's turmoil when he defies God, who is covered in its immutable silence. The stanzas have between six and nine syllables each: by its rhythm and length, the next to last stanza is the climax of the poet's revolt against the absurdity of God, that he calls "the Great Unknown". The last "verse" is the shortest and becomes the expression of appeasement, of the poet's mystic abandonment and powerless feeling when faced with the ineffable side life. The translation should preserve these formal features of the source text in such a way that the French reader could "come across the Other" and enjoy the diversity of the other language, according to Antoine Berman (1999: 84).

We notice that the beginning of the poet's mystic confession is differently treated by the two translators:

"O durere totdeauna mi-a fost singurătatea ta ascunsă. Dumnezeule, dar ce era să fac? Când eram copil mă jucam cu tine. Și-n închipuire te desfăceam cum desfaci o jucărie."	"Ta solitude cachée m'a toujours fait souffrir. Seigneur, mais que pouvais-je faire? Enfant, je jouais avec toi. Je te démontais par l'imagination comme on bride un jouet."[10]	"Une douleur me fut toujours ta solitude cachée, mais, mon Dieu, qu'aurais-je pu faire? Quand j'étais enfant je jouais avec toi. Et dans mon imagination te démontais comme l'on démonte un jouet."[11]

The poet's soliloquy begins with a rhetorical question that the translators prefer to interpret following their own exegesis. While the phrase "solitude cachée" is translated literally in order to suggest the "coffin" ("cercueil") in which God hid himself, the turns taken by the interrogation in French are different. We consider that the translation signed by Ștefana and Ioan Pop-Curșeu is too literal and, in a certain way, exaggerated compared with the structure of the French phrase. On the contrary, the first translator chose the verb "to suffer" ("souffrir") to suggest "the pain" ("la douleur") described in the source text. The choice of the verbal tenses is another element revealing the diversity that marks the source text: "le passé simple" that we find in the second translation contributes to render the target text more poetical, method which we mentioned previously in our study. The despair suggested by the question addressed to the Great Unknown who seems dumb is expressed by "l'imparfait", but also by "le conditionnel passé"

---

10   Translated from Romanian by Sanda Stolojan, *L'étoile la plus triste*, 1992.
11   Translated from Romanian by Ștefana and Ioan Pop-Curșeu, in Lucian Blaga, *Poèmes*, suivi de Nichita Stănescu, *Une Vision des Sentiments*, 2003.

which, in our opinion, emphasized the irreversibility of the lost time. Concerning the comparison between the effort to comprehend God (called by Blaga "luciferic knowledge", "connaissance luciférienne" in French) and the childish game, the translators have, again, the liberty of choice: while the former avoids to repeat the verb "to dismantle" ("démonter", in French) and introduces an ellipsis ("enfant, je jouais avec toi"), the latter, in her effort to be faithful to the original text, prefers to translate literally the semantic content, respecting, at the same time, the formal level.

We find then one of the beautiful enumerations specific to Blaga's style:

"... și fără să-mi fi fost vreodată aproape, te-am pierdut pentru totdeauna, în țărână, în foc, în văzduh și pe ape."	"... et sans t'avoir jamais sentir proche, je t'ai perdu pour toujours, dans la terre et le feu, sur les eaux et dans les aires."	"... et sans que jamais tu m'eusses été proche, Je t'ai perdu pour toujours, Dans la terre, dans le feu, dans l'air et sur les eaux."

The enumeration is an important stylistic device of Blaga's poetic style, as the poet confesses that he loves "flowers and eyes, lips and tombs" ("les fleurs et les yeux, les lèvres et les tombes").[12] This time, we notice that the first translator decided to group the terms of the enumeration for rhythmical reasons. We also notice in case of the second translation "le subjonctif passé" that weighs the French phrase down. There is also a subtle rhyme linking the first and the last verse in Romanian. Unfortunately, this rhyme could not be preserved in the target language, but it is compensated by the preservation of poetic features and the creation of the inner rhythm in translation.

A major problem that the translator may find in Lucian Blaga's poetic work is the transposition of metaphor, especially of the extended metaphor:

"Între răsăritul de soare și apusul de soare sunt numai tină și rană. În cer te-ai închis ca-ntr-un coșciug."	"De l'aube au crépuscule. Je ne suis que fange et blessure. Toi, tu t'es enfermé dans ton ciel comme dans un cercueil."	"Entre le soleil qui se lève et celui qui décline. Je ne suis plus que plaie et fange. Comme dans un cercueil tu t'es enfermé dans le ciel."

The poet's philosophic conception is another sign of the diversity that characterizes his work. We have here a double metaphoric game meant to suggest the mystic sense of the human being and the decline after the fall from Heaven. The man who lost paradise gained the power of purifying creation, but he feels alie-

---

[12] Je ne foule pas la corolle de merveilles du monde, translated from Romanian by Sanda Stolojan, in L'étoile la plus triste, 1992.

nated from his Creator. The temporal limits of the human turmoil are understood differently by the two translators, as the former chooses a more concise formula ("De l'aube au crepuscule / Je ne suis que fange et blessure"). On the other hand, we find in the second translation an inversion of the lexemes that form the metaphor, used to preserve the rhyme of the verses, in other words, for formal reasons. Thus, the balance between form and content is preserved in translation.

The emphasis of poetic features and the recreation are, in our opinion, translation techniques that may help the translator to deal with diversity. In this case, the translators resort to the recreation of the iconic structure in order to "paint" this God who hides himself in his sky as in a coffin. The former translation is more emphatic, (due to the use of the pronoun "toi" and of the possessive adjective "ton ciel" that becomes a device of the translator). The latter, more literal, contains a turn of phrase emphasizing the Nietzschean image of the coffin. In this immobile universe, God is the supreme absence, and the translators choose the same technique to "paint" this isolation of divinity: "Oh, si tu n'étais plus apparenté à la mort / qu'à la vie, / tu me parlerais."

Then we find metaphors that send us to the biblical semantic field. The translation of these metaphors in the target language is a literal one: "les épines d'ici-bas", "la lance envenimée". One may also notice the rhyme in the following fragment:

"Eşti muta, neclintita identitate (rotunjit în sine a este a) Nu ceri nimic. Nici măcar rugăciunea mea."	"Tu est l'immuable, l'identité muette (arrondi en soi a est a) Tu ne demandes rien, pas même une prière."	"Tu es l'immuable, muette identité (arrondi sur lui-même a est a) Tu ne demandes rien. Pas même une prière de moi."

Apart from the different translation of the "appeasing" epithet, specific to Blaga's style (Bârlea, in *L'ontologie de la souffrance chez Lucian Blaga*, 2004:34), which has here strong philosophic connotations, ("l'immuable, muette identité"), we may notice, in case of the second version, the translator's effort to preserve the rhyme from the source text, fact that is, in our opinion, outstanding. Once again, the balance between form and content, together with the diversity of the source text, are preserved in the target language, as the translator chooses to emphasize the poetic features of the original text.

Further on, we prefer the structure "mes interrogatives tristesses" instead of "mes questionneuses tristesses", that we consider clumsy. We may also notice that the metaphor "Iată e noapte fără ferestre-n afară", expressing the human being's climax of anxiety in front of God's silence, is more adequately translated by the former translator ("La nuit est sans fenêtres sur le monde") compared to the latter ("Voilà, il fait nuit sans fenêtres vers le dehors", the term "le dehors" being, in fact, too vague).

It seems that the key-metaphor of the poem and one of the touchstones for the translator is the final one:

| "Dumnezeule, de-acum ce mă fac? În mijlocul tău mă dezbrac. Mă dezbrac de trup ca de-o haină pe care-o lași în drum." | "Seigneur, désormais que vais-je devenir? Laisse-moi me défaire en toi, me dépouiller de mon corps comme d'un vêtement abandonné en route." | "Mon Dieu, que deviendrai-je désormais? Dans ton cœur je me déshabille. Je me déshabille de mon corps comme d'un vêtement qu'on laisse sur son chemin." |

It is the metaphor of the abandonment in the very nature of the divinity; it is the supreme revelation of the inability to grasp the hidden senses only with the help of the "luciferic knowledge". The poet's choice is to abandon his material being and live at the heart of mysteries. In this sense, it is interesting to notice the presence of the verb "to become" ("devenir") in the two versions, verb that expresses the continuous flow of time and the decay of the material world. The Great Unknown is called sometimes "Seigneur", sometimes "mon Dieu", fact that reflects a different exegesis of the translator. The poet "undresses himself" ("se dishabille") in the very essence of the divine and gives up his material body. This metaphor of the self abandonment, that we may consider a mark of the diversity characterizing the source text, is built in the target language on the verbs "se dépouiller" and "se défaire", and on the repetition of the verb "se déshabiller". On the other hand, the comparison of the human body to clothing is rendered literally in the translation.

There is, presumably, a loss in the poetic text concerning the semantic selection at the contextual level, selection that is meant to facilitate comprehension. The differences caused by linguistic habits and by "the materiality of the linguistic sign" (Meschonnic) do not prevent translation. The transposition in the source language is carried out at the semantic, morphologic and syntactic levels, but also at the formal level, as the inner rhythm of the verses and the structure of the poem are preserved in the target text.

3. Concluding remarks

We may call "materiality of the linguistic sign" the set of semantic, phonic, morphemic, lexical and syntactic features, but also of formal features analyzed as they are expressed in the source text and dealt with in an adequate way in the target text. In this sense, "poetry is not more "difficult" to translate than "prose", claims Henri

Meschonnic (1972: 53); this so-called difficulty is the result of the conception that poetry is a "violation of the linguistic norms", instead of an expression of diversity at several levels. One strategy for translating poetic texts and revealing their diversity is, according to Meschonnic, the preservation of poetic features or "literarisation" of content, both resulting from an "aesthetic ideology" (1972: 54). In this context, any translation of a poetic text is rewriting of the source text with the means of the target language, as "plus la traduction de la poéticité du texte est réussie, plus la part de réécriture est importante; plus on est fidèle au texte d'origine, c'est à dire moins la traduction de la poéticité est réussie, mois la part de réécriture est importante" (Radhouane, 2000).[13] The only demand is the adequacy of content and the respect for the form; as for the rest, the translator is free to choose the strategies that he considers appropriate in order to express in the target language the linguistic and cultural diversity of the source language and to "pick" the fruit of the poem.

References

Primary sources

Lucian Blaga. 1992. *L'étoile la plus triste*, translated by Sanda Stolojan, Paris: Orphée, La Différence.
Lucian Blaga. 2003. *Poèmes, suivi de Nichita Stănescu, Une Vision des Sentiments*, excerpts, translated by Ștefana and Ioan Pop-Curșeu, Paris: Autres Temps.

Secondary sources

Bârlea, Gheorghe. 2004. "Les échelons du silence dans la poésie de Lucian Blaga", in *L'ontologie de la souffrance chez Lucian Blaga*, edited by Horia Bădescu, *Cahiers bleus*, Troyes.
Berman, Antoine. 1999. La traduction de la lettre ou L'auberge du lointain, Paris: Seuil.

---

13 "(...) the more successful the translation of a poetic text is, the more important is the rewriting; the more faithful to the source text we are, in other words, the less successful is the translation of a poetic text, is, the less important is the rewriting" (our translation).

Jakobson, Roman. 1975. « Aspectos lingüísticos da traduçao », in: *Lingüística e comuniçao*, translated by Isidoro Blikstein and José Paulo Paes, São Paulo: São Paulo Cultrix.

Jakobson, Roman. 2003. *Essais de linguistique générale*, Paris: Éditions Minuit.

Kibédi-Varga, Aron. 1979. Les constants du poème, analyse du langage poétique, Paris: Flammarion.

Ladmiral, Jean-René. 1979. *Traduire, théorème pour la traduction*, Paris: Petite Bibliothèque Payot.

Meschonnic, Henri, *Propositions pour une poétique de la traduction*, 1972. Available online: http://www.persee.fr/web/revues/home/prescript/article/ lgge_0458-726x_1972_num_7_28_2097. Accessed 12 October 2010.

Pergnier, Maurice. 1999. « La traduction comme exégèse: le cas de la poésie », in « TTR: traduction, terminologie, rédaction », vol. 12, no. 2.

Radhouane, Nebil. 2000. « Saint-John Perse: le paradoxe de l'hermétisme et de la traductibilité », dans *Meta*, 45-3, special number *« La traduction dans le monde arabe »*.

Translation from Gallo to French in Brittany's Hospitals: Views about Methodology and Epistemology

Clément Ferré

Thinking (and putting it in writing) in a language that is not our first language can lead to linguistic insecurity, enhanced by the fact that the linguistic socialisation in this language is not appropriated to the linguistic skills required by the different situations. We talk about a universal case, that is a characteristic of the urban context stimulating spatial mobility, anonymity and loosening social relationships, in refering to the School of Chicago[1]. This context enables the meeting of linguistic and anthropological otherness that includes the development of new pedagogical and cultural politics to create new social links.

The title of this meeting, *Translation and the Accommodation of Diversity*, even though it is a discursive expression which can be adjusted to different ages for various countries, it is more than ever a topical question because of the multicultural crisis (according to the viewpoints of political leaders of Germany, Angela Merkel – October the 16th 2010 –, Great Britain, David Cameron – February the 5th 2011 – and France, Nicolas Sarkozy – February the 10th 2011 – who said the multiculturalism has failed[2]), new questions about immigration and the economic development of new emerging countries. The world economic, political and demographic reconfiguration requires new perspectives to host and accomodate the different anthropological life styles, between the French assimilation (one citizenship = one culture) and the Anglo-Saxon communautarianism (different communities identified as cultural communities do not live together). Because of this new ideological situation about an old social situation, new multicultural problems emerge in France; it includes all aspects of all anthropological otherness like local cultures and local languages. We hope this sociolinguistic analyze give birth to new interrogations about multiculturalism.

In social situations where the language is a capital like coal, tools and machine[3], linguistic and cultural diversity is an important element to create signification and common meaning between different people. Thanks to a sociolinguistic epistemology and methodology, it is possible to analyze, understand and explain

---

1   Coulon A., 2002, 28.
2   In *Le Monde,* February the 25th 2011, 19.
3   Boutet J., 2008, 89.

the process and the link between French linguistic politics, sociolinguistic representations, language at work and the meaning construction in interactions including different languages and cultures that seem similar because of the linguistic politics of the French State. And because of this French linguistic politics and of the linguistic ideology, translation was confined to "great" and "true" languages like English, German, Spanish, Italian and it was not applied to social languages and local languages. It seems that the social demand keeps on increasing regarding all variations and sociolinguistic differences in social life and specially in professional life. This is one of the scientific reasons why we were eager to analyze the different links between linguistic diversity (of near languages), translation, accomodation and language at work in hospital with the therapeutic work.

As a sociolinguistic work, we consider the fact that "linguistic politics" is a simplistic expression to fully understand the ins and outs of such a situation. Here we prefer the concept of "glottopolitic" which was developed by the French sociolinguist Jean-Baptise Marcellesi. It means that everyone, every group and every institution produce sociolinguistic norms (descriptions, prescriptions, proscriptions) in many different situations. Linguistic politics are not exclusive to political State in national space, sociolinguistic norms are different, sometimes in conflict. In a sociolinguistic research we cannot put aside metalinguistic discourses of people who are the first concerened. The communication is more complicated than the "sender – receiver" pattern. The meaning of the original message and the meaning of the social reception can be very different, due to the different social positions of people which include different media and ways of appropriation.

But more than a description of the sociolinguistic situation, we only consider the concept of "glottopolitic" as useful if it is correlated to another one: the concept of "glottonomy":

> "This concept means the importance of the analysis of linguistic practices to be followed by a reflection and social action about modalities of an intervention on this linguistic practices"[4].

So, this sociolinguistic analysis has for purpose an applied sociolinguistic which has to have an effect on clarified items including: defining what Gallo is, by whom it is speaken in Brittany's hospitals, defining language at work in hospitals, defining what we mean by translation between close languages and clarifiying which referents have to be "transformed" into vocal sounds and as a result, translating if any people need it.

---

4   Free translation of: « Ce dernier terme pose entre autres la nécessité de faire suivre l'analyse des pratiques langagières d'une réflexion et partant d'une action sur les modalités d'une intervention sur ces mêmes pratiques » (Bulot T., 2006, 51).

What do we mean by Gallo?

French linguistic diversity is one of the most important of the West Europe[5] but only one is recognized by the Constitution: French. It can be understood through the history of the French Republic construction illustrating the fact that republicans have considered and nowadays still consider French to get hold of the French citizenship. During the French Revolution, other languages were suspected of being vehicles of the Reaction and of the Ancien Regime but nothing has been done to teach French to the new French people and to eradicate other languages (due to the civil war and political twitches).

The most representative French linguistic politics eras are the ones that has been undertaken during the Third (1870-1940) and the Fourth (1946-1958) Republics thanks to the school and the consolidation of the national market with the technical linguistic normalization. The French "assimilation" politics have relegated other native languages to private space (especially in family) but not with coercive measures (just some cases at school but they were overestimated by linguistic campaigners) neither with the impossibility to communicate with civil servants who worked in public services. If French has succeeded to become the only language of France, it is because people who did not speak French were agreed not to transmit their language to their children due to the fact that the French Republic was seen as a progresvve institution that enabled to escape poverty and the Catholic Church influence. Consequently, French was seen as a way to escape this poverty. Moreover, the Catholic Church preaches were said in local languages, so it brought French Republic discourses to associate, again, local languages with the Reaction and religious fundamentalism and obscurantism. Today, due to the urban system domination, local languages are described as rural languages which carries on continue the devaluation started during the 18th century.

But after the Second World War, many people got involved in cultural associations to reassert the value of local languages because most of them had observed a breach in the familial transmission process due to the shame of oneself and the importance of diglossia situations[6]. The demand process is pretty simultaneous with the ones regarding languages and cultures inherited from the African workers immigration (from old colonies). But the main difference is that people who spoke languages inherited from immigration suffered less from shame because most of their languages are recognized in other countries and if not, they are socially recognized (like popular Arabic). It usually is not the case for local

---

5   Breton R., 2003, 48.
6   Marcellesi J-B., 2003, (1979), 119.

languages and especially for local languages of the north of France (Oïl languages), just like Gallo.

In Brittany, Breton (a Celtic language) is traditionnaly spoken in the west of the country and Gallo in the east (the linguistic line goes from the city of Saint-Brieuc to the city of Vannes). The INSEE (National Institute of Statistics and Economic Studies – France) gives the number in 1999, of 28 300 Gallo speakers and 200 000 Breton speakers[7]. A quick glance at the situation thanks to discurses about the linguistic situation in Brittany enables us to understand that Breton actually stands in a better place than Gallo. If it is true about social representations, it is probably not true about transmission and practices.

As far as social representations are concerned, Gallo, unlike Breton, is not considered as a self-sufficient language but as a French dialect ("patois" in French and in most cases, Gallo speakers do not use the glossonym Gallo because this name comes from the north-west of the Gallo area and has been taken up by a linguistic movement. Consequently the rest of Gallo speakers think Gallo is another language or that their Gallo is a deficient form of the "true" Gallo in the north-west), it is depreciated by politicians and by Gallo speakers themselves.

But Gallo has probably known a better transmission than Breton. In fact, the number of Gallo speakers is probably the same (or a little superior) as the one of Breton speakers and in this case:

> "it says Gallo keeps a social anchoring not necessarily perceptible from the outside, but it allows Gallo to be really alive in many places"[8].

Despite the fact that Gallo is underestimated compared to Breton, it has benefited from its structural similarity with the hegemonic language in the French social space, which is French. Gallo speakers, most of the time, do not think they use two different languages (unlike Breton, Corsican, Basque, Alsatian, Flesmish and some local Oc languages). They probably less feel a normative pressure to do sociolinguistic backwards and forwards. Some sociolinguists say local Oïl languages "have been transmitted at 25% and Breton at 10%"[9].

Gallo can be an element in some areas for therapeutic communication situations in hospitals in Brittany.

---

7   Insee, 1999, 1.
8   Free translation of: « C'est dire que la langue gallèse conserve un ancrage social pas forcément très perceptible de l'extérieur, mais qui lui permet, en de nombreux lieux, d'être encore vraiment vivante » (Agoujard J-P., Manzano F., 2008, 7).
9   Manzano F., 2003, 137.

Hospital Work and Otherness

All care activities and relationships come along the meeting between identity and otherness. Concerning identity it is because we are human beings and we share common medical problems and universal human rights. As for otherness it is because diversity has became a norm in modern societies and a primordial element in political and social problems.

"Cultural diversity is often linked to linguistic diversity which included codes plurality used in modern societies, which are all multilingual in various degrees"[10]. Medical care and hospital work need unity between identity and otherness, which is always fragile, "treat or being treated always requires with uncertainty, a meeting unity, between an action and a word"[11].

A care relationship involves inter-personal skills, engaged in a relation with another human being, which is very particularly and entails a blatant dissymmetry between the medical staff ("Subjects supposed to know" as the psychanalyst Jacques Lacan said) and the patient, vulnerable and fragile who is here to be helped. This relationship situation creates asymmetric interactions where distress reveals a break in the patient's world informality, and it can disorientates brutally the patient. And "in this case, illness does not only modify our world environment, it can change our world perception"[12].

To receive, understand and translate the patient problems in a scientific way, the medical staff needs words but unfortunately, occidental medicine in its majority, has developed the idea of considering language as a tool to translate pathological sounds into medical language. In this situation, the patient language, which expresses the patient subjectivity, is seen as an obstacle that can parasite the pathological message. Good pre-requisites for a global human care consist in

> "avoiding the patient reification, it means his transformation into a knowledge object or into a self-fullfilment way [...]. The other features and claims simplification often is the first step of dehumanization because it ascribes inhuman trappings to human being made of flesh and blood"[13].

---

10 Free translation of: « Elle [la diversité culturelle] va souvent de pair avec la diversité linguistique qui indique la pluralité des codes employés dans les sociétés modernes, lesquelles sont toutes multilingues à des degrés divers » (Guidere M., 2010a, 21).

11 Free translation of: « Soigner ou être soigné, c'est toujours solliciter, dans l'incertitude et la fragilité, l'unité d'une rencontre, d'un geste, d'une parole » (Lombard J., Vandewalle B., 2010, 76).

12 Free translation of: « En ce sens, la maladie ne fait pas que modifier les éléments de notre rapport au monde; elle est ce qui peut changer notre rapport même au monde » (Lombard J., Vandewalle B., 2010, 77).

13 Free translation of: « Ensuite, il faut éviter la chosification de l'autre c'est-à-dire sa transformation en objet de connaissance ou en moyen d'accomplissement personnel [...]. La simplification des traits et des revendications de l'autre est souvent le premier pas vers la déshumanisation

Obviously, medical care implies an intersubjectivity dimension which resists to technicist approaches. These subjectivities appear when anthropological and linguistic distance is too big or too far away. But what can these subjectivities signify? We understand, thanks to anthropology, that human attitudes, expressions and comportments can culturally be placed. In a medical environment, attitudes, expressions and comportments, can be, for who knows how to decode them, a psychic suffering discourse. But a psychological discourse is not a cultural discourse, it is, at the very most, a screen behind the psychological problem. Some medical researchers have borrowed a primordial assumption: illness and culture are closely linked. To truly help a patient, the medical staff needs to know how illness and culture(s) (including social class culture) are based on a patient, the concept of "decentration" can really be hopeful here:

> "In decentration, changing views must enable to have a better perception of a situation, to have new perspectives through others to appreciate much better their point of view (representations, feelings, attitudes)"[14].

An effective treatment supposes that medical person and the patient understand each other, when not, it is possible to call an interpreter but the experience shows that the results depend on situations and they may be very variable. Some signification gap and comprehension differences can appear even with the same signifiers. Problems in a relationship betwenn the medical person and the patient in a multicultural situation are more elaborated than linguistic problems, they are structural problems. For example, two people (a medical doctor and a patient) who talk, with the same signifiers, about eye trouble, can speak about different pathological problems. In the occidental scientific culture, eye trouble means eye trouble, "but in some traditional medicine cultures, eye trouble can mean sexual trouble"[15]. Or, in Gallo of Fougères (city in the east of Brittany), when a woman says "je n'i vouès pus" ("I can't see anymore" in French), she means she does not have her periods anymore. In Gallo, a way of saying "I can't see anymore" is "je n'i vouès goute"[16].

Cultural subjectivities and linguistic diversity is an important element because we are aware of the close link between the psychological dimension of the patient and the state of the health evolution. The treatment effectiveness also depends on the global atmosphere when the treatment is given and taken.

---

parce qu'elle revient à prêter des attributs inhumains (d'objets ou d'animaux) à des êtres de chair et de sang » (Guidere M., 2010b, 208).

14 Free translation of: « Dans la décentration, il s'agit de changer de perspective afin de mieux percevoir une situation, de se placer dans l'optique d'autrui afin de mieux apprécier son point de vue (représentations, émotions, attitudes) » (Guidere M., 2010, 34).

15 Snacken J., 1991, 8.

16 Aufray R., 2007, 970.

The global care atmosphere can change through the multiplication of verbal interactions between the medical staff and the patient, notably for the adaptation of the patient in the medical structure which is a source of stress. This kind of interaction is called "long-transactions", they are more than care actions and include an exchange of anthropological information. These "long-transactions" are otherness meetings which require some translation and accomodation for the medical staff.

Collateral languages and Translation

We are reusing here the concept of "collateral languages" which has been elaborated during a conference that took place in 2001, in Amiens in France (edited by Jean-Michel Eloy in 2004 entitled *Des langues collatérales. Problèmes linguistiques, sociolinguistiques et glottopolitiques de la proximité linguistique*, L'Harmattan, Paris) and has defined the concept as

> "refering to linguistic, sociolinguistic and historic or glottopolitic closely related languages (objectively and subjectively). The closely related languages are seen as historically linked by their terms of development"[17].

Linguistic proximity is seen here through a dynamic and sociopolitical perspective that helps us to understand a sociolinguistic language dynamic considered through all languages it is connected to, linguistically or socially speaking. For example, links between Corsican and Italian have evolved. Fifty years ago, Corsican was considered as an Italian dialect, but today it is a self-sufficient language. It implies many translating consequences.

With this concept, we can see that the Roman Jakobson typology is not a guided by a scientific mind but by ideology. Jakobson typology is:

> "1. Intralingual translation or rewording consists in a linguistic signs interpretation or with other signs from the same language.
> 2. Interlingual translation or translation as such consists in a linguistic signs interpretation with another language.
> 3. Intersmiotic translation or transmutation consists in a linguistic signs interpretation with non linguistic signs systems"[18].

---

17 Free translation of: « Nous proposons de désigner par ‹ langues collatérales › des variétés proches – objectivement et subjectivement –, aux plans linguistique, sociolinguistique et historique ou glottopolitique, les variétés tendanciellement en contraste étant historiquement liées par les modalités de leur développement » (Eloy J-M., 2007, 20).

18 Free translation of:
« 1. La traduction intralinguale ou reformulation consiste en l'interprétation des signes linguistiques au moyen d'autres signes de la même langue.

This typology is a relative tool which depends on a political linguistic situation, for example, with Corsican and Italian again, fifty years ago, translating Italian to Corsican was considered as an intralingual translation. But today, Corsican is, objectively and subjectively, a self-sufficient language. As a result, translating Italian to Corsican is now an interlingual translation.

And what is a problem in intralingual translation definition, which is rewording, is the fact that as a common meaning it can just mean a simple adaptation, another lexical choice which does not require an outside help because someone who does not manage to get understood can be described as a bad-speaker. It is something commonly to heard about Gallo speakers: "they don't need any translation, they need to learn how to speak good French" or "what they say is nonsens".

What is here depends on two attitudes: class or otherness contempt or the reification signification in words. What we need here is more linguistic relativism, in this connection Wittgenstein said:

> "never forget that words have no other signification that the one we give them, their significations are conferred by our explanations. [...] Philosophers often talk about searching and analyzing the meaning of words. But they remind us that the words significations only come from us, they do not come from an independent power, as a result we can scientifically establish what a word really means. A word has the signification that someone gave it"[19].

The possibility to see into a message or a word comes from the fact that:

> "it is easy to imagine we have given a meaning to a word, when in reality we did not, when we use it in a similar combination – which unfortunately is a superficially and deceptive similarity – to familiar contexts where the word already has a meaning"[20].

The linguistic otherness can partly come from some linguistic practices seeming "unnatural" or meaningless because they are in between proximity (same signifiers) and the unknown (different signifieds). But the same signifiers can have different signifieds if people had different ways of socialization.

---

2. La traduction interlinguale ou traduction proprement dite consiste en l'interprétation des signes linguistiques au moyen d'une autre langue.
3. La traduction intersémiotique ou transmutation consiste en l'interprétation des signes linguistiques au moyen de systèmes de signes non linguistiques » (Jakobson R., 193, 79).

19 Free translation of: « N'oubliez jamais que les mots n'ont d'autres signification que celle que vous leur avez donnée, et ce sens là ils le tiennent de nos explication. [...] Les philosophes parlent très souvent de chercher, analyser le sens des mots. Mais souvenons-nous que c'est nous qui avons donné leur sens aux mots, qu'ils ne le tiennent pas d'une puissance indépendante; ainsi nous est-il possible de procéder à une enquête scientifique sur la signification réelle d'un mot. Un mot a le sens qui lui est donné par quelqu'un » (Wittgenstein L., 1965, 84 and 85).

20 Free translation of: « L'illusion provient du fait qu'il est facile de s'imaginer que l'on a donné un sens à un mot, bien qu'en réalité on ne l'ait pas fait, lorsqu'on l'utilise dans une combinaison qui ressemble – mais ne ressemble malheureusement que de façon superficielle et trompeuse – à des contextes familiers dans lesquels il en a déjà un » (Bouveresse J., 1997, 121).

Futhermore it is important to consider that languages are not only linguistic systems, they are a complex social reality, including linguistic elements, but also practical conceptions, representations and institutionalization which fixe language in relation to social struggles. Jean-Michel Eloy suggests to separate linguistic elements from social and psychological elements, a typology which

> "depends on two standards:
> a) Linguistic connections, to precise "genetic distance" between different varieties.
> b) Individuation, like social and political consensus about the existence of two different languages"[21].

According to this typology, we can place Gallo, compared to French in a low distinction. Linguistic proximity is maximal and there are some debates on the fact that Gallo and French can be two different languages. The consideration of Gallo being a self-sufficient language is in progress (like other sociolinguistic situations as for Scots and English, Aragonian and Spanish, etc.).

And instead of viewing the linguistic proximity as a clue of "bad derivative language" which has to be corrected, it is possible to see this proximity as a translation and and intercomprehension way. Gallo and French share very close phonological systems, syntaxic systems and common lexical bases. Through this proximity it is possible to develop some real multilingual skills for medical staff.

Translation is a real communicating skill, especially to communicate with others no matter how culturally and linguistically close they are. In his famous speech adressed in 1813 (June the 24th), called *Of different ways to translate*, Friedrich Schleiermacher said different varieties from of a same language are already "different languages which often require a complete oral transposition" and many situations require reformulations "between contemporary people who are separated by dialects and belong to different popular classes"[22].

This all leads us to believe translation is an otherness accomodation with different degrees of known and unknown linguistic and cultural elements. Schleiermacher teaches us that translation is a question of difficulty because translating a foreign literary work or all linguistic productions into the "hosted

---

21   Free translation of:
      « a) La parente, i-e l'existence d'une même variété ascendante, dont on pourra préciser la « distance génétique ».
      b) L'individuation, i-e l'existence d'un consensus socio-politique (objectivable en discours et objectivé par des institutions) sur l'existence de deux langues distinctes » (Eloy J-M., 2007, 24).

22   Free translation of: « Des langues différentes exigeant souvent une transposition orale complète », « des contemporains qui ne sont déparés par le dialecte et qui appartiennent à des classes populaires différentes » (Schleiermacher F., 1999, 31).

language" strenghtenes difficulties already met in our own culture and language every time that there is a kind of distance inside a discourse.

What are the differences between interpretation and translation? We reuse here the thesis of the French philosopher François Ost who said:

> "these two operations have the same goal: signs comprehension, but taking the problem by two opposite entries, interpretation is deploying with an almost assured precomprehension form (there is always preliminary harmony), while translation is always struggled, in contrary, with the non translatable obstacle and with any form of complicity"[23].

It is important to understand this point of view through a dialectic vision and skepticism. The precomprehension form can take the appearance of a similarity veil and there can be some common elements in uncertainty of translation. *Via* this dynamic vision of internal and external translation, we believe it allows to recognize translation and interpretation skills in the medical staff, to reveal passive potentialities, particularly the capacity of recognizing, thanks to professional experiences, linguistic and cultural otherness when ideology says there is no.

Which Reality to Translate?

As we said before, translating means that there are some common elements between people, at least about referents because "we precisely live in one world, not two neither three nor seventeen ones"[24], this world is partly formed by physical elements "already-here" about our words confirming us their existence, but they exist without us. What about the status of medical referents? It is more complex than talking about physical elements like mountains or grass (it is established that they exist without us), because illness and medical problems cannot exist without us (it is a tautology to say it but it is important) and yet, we do not put our intentionality into them. But medical and patient discourses are not neutral or totally objective because of subjectivities (we already said it) but also because of a global life theology which can be objectivized and then, translate into a human symbolic and common system of linguistic signs.

---

23 Free translation of: « Les deux opérations visent le même enjeu: la compréhension de signes, mais prennent pour ainsi dire le problème par deux bouts opposés, l'interprétation se déployant sur fond de précompréhension assurée, du moins pressentie (il y a toujours déjà « entente préalable »), tandis que la traduction ne cesse de se débattre, au contraire, avec l'obstacle de l'intraduisible et ne s'autorise d'aucune forme de complicité à priori » (Ost F., 2009, 137).

24 Free translation of: « Nous vivons très exactement dans un monde, pas dans deux ou trois ou dix-sept » (Searle J. R., 2008, 9).

Although illness is partly formed of material form, it is important to distinguish it from other material forms which John Searle calls "raw facts" like:

> "the fact that the Everest Mountain has snow and ice in its top, or the fact that hydrogen atoms only have one electron: here are facts that totally independent of any human opinion"[25].

In spite of the fact that illness cannot be classified with raw facts, it can be classified with "institutional facts" like the fact that a piece of paper can be a twenty Euro note. "Institutional facts are called like this because they need human institutions to exist"[26]. Illness does not need medical institution to exist but it can exist without human beings. Of course, illness needs the medical and language institution to be pronounced, but the pronounced fact has to be distinguished from its utterance.

As a matter of fact, the illness enunciation and its different translations can accept what we call "social relativity of descriptions" which can be defined as:

> "the plan we adopt to describe that the world depends, in fact, on the one we think useful to adopt; and the plan we think useful to adopt depends, in fact, on needs and contingent interests that, as social human beings, we have"[27].

But accepting this social relativity of descriptions did not lead us to what we call "the dependance of things concernings descriptions" which can be defined like this:

> "All facts necessarily depend on a description: there cannot be any fact question about things that exist in the world unconnected to our propensity to describe the world as being in a way. It is when we have adopted a plan to describe the world that there are facts concerning the world" [28].

An example can illustrate this point. Through the common notion of "object" that we have, there are three objects (called X1, X2 and X3). Hilary Putman, in *Realism With a Human Face* (published in 1990), invites us to think differently from

---

25 Free translation of: « Des faits tels que le mont Everest a de la neige et de la glace près de son sommet, ou que les atomes d'hydrogène n'ont qu'un électron: voilà des faits totalement indépendants de toute opinion humaine » (Searle J. R., 1998, 13).
26 Free translation of: « Les faits institutionnels sont appelés ainsi parce qu'ils ont impérativement besoin d'institutions humaines pour exister » (Searle J. R., 1998, 14).
27 Free translation of: « Le schème que nous adoptons pour décrire le monde dépend, en définitive, du schème que nous trouvons utile d'adopter: et le schème que nous trouvons utile d'adopter dépend, en définitive, des besoins et intérêts contingents que nous avons en tant qu'êtres sociaux » (Boghossian P., 2009, 37).
28 Free translation of: « Tous les faits dépendent nécessairement d'une description: il ne peut y avoir de question de fait quant à la façon dont les choses sont dans le monde indépendamment de notre propension à décrire le monde comme étant d'une certaine façon. C'est une fois que nous avons adopté un certain schéma pour décrire le monde qu'il commence à y avoir des faits concernant le monde » (Boghossian P., 2009, 36).

our common sense and imagines that every group of two particulars gives a new thing that is the result of their association. Consequently, there are not three things anymore, but seven (X1; X2: X3; X1+X2; X1+X3; X2+X3; X1+X2+X3). With this argument Putman says there is no objectivity and things living without a description plan. On the contrary, it is an argument in favor of objectivity because the two answers (three and seven) both are correct. Indeed the two arguments have two different object conceptions but what Paul Boghossian called "base facts" (here the three or seven things) are the same and then, they can accept different descriptions and translations all equally true or corresponding.

To establish what characterizes some world referents, we need a typology which clearly defines the concepts of objectivity and subjectivity.

"Concerning this current discussion, two meanings are decisive, an epistemic meaning of objective-subjective distinction and an ontological meaning"[29].

The epistemic one refers to judgment predicates which depend on attitudes. For example, enouncing "French is better than Gallo" refers to an epistemic subjectivity, but enouncing "the majority of Gallo speakers have a linguistic insecurity" refers to an epistemic objectivity because facts corresponding to an epistemic objective utterance do not depend on attitudes and feelings. The ontological meaning refers to entities predicates which enables ways of existence. For example, pains are subjective entities because they need human beings to exist. On the contrary, mountains are ontologically objectives because their way of existence is totally independent from any subject or mental state.

In a medical application, we can fully understand health states or utterance like "Right now I am having a backache", it is refers to an epistemic objective fact because it is linked to a fact which does not depend on attitudes or human opinions. Nevertheless, the phenomenon itself, the real pain, has a subjective way of existence.

But knowing that there are common referents in a medical interaction does not mean what their common referents are, even more if interactions are produced in two different languages (close or not, we talk about different ways of signification). Like what has been shown in *Word and Object* (published in 1960 by Quine), it is difficult, when the signification ways are very different, to establish an indisputable matter of fact that would enable to choose between different translations. Agreeing about a referent (or imagining that we agree on a referent) is not enough to facilitate mutual understanding. Knowing different global language structures is also important to understand each other in a medical interaction.

---

29 Free translation of: « Pour la discussion qui nous occupe, deux sens sont décisifs, un sens épistémique de la distinction objectif-subjectif et un sens ontologique » (Searle J. R., 1998, 21).

Conclusion

At this point, we have shown two elements that could enable the medical staff (and the French society) to develop new ways to welcome (care after) Gallo speaker patients: a sociolinguistic one and a socio-symbolic one.

The first one consists in the importance of knowing the referential, signification and linguistic system of others in order to develop an intercomprehension in medical interactions when linguistic and anthropological otherness is present. Therefore, though a doctorate work, we hope to contribute to the creation of new linguistic tools (like vocabulary book for medical doctors or nurses) and offer new formations to nurses about the instauration of a communication with patients in close but nevertheless different languages.

The second one refers to a new linguistic otherness view, which clearly is the opposite of the French linguistic ideology. We are here reusing the concept of "polynomic language" which was developed by Jean-Baptiste Marcellesi and that can be defined as:

> "a polynomic language is a language with an abstract unity, speakers recognize that it has several ways of existing. They are all equally tolerated and there is no hierarchy nor functions specialization between them. A polynomic language goes together with intertolerance between different varieties of speakers on phonological and morphological plans; moreover, the lexical multiplicity is seen as a richness element"[30].

The concept of a polynomic language could become the "spirit" of these new nurses formations that we fight for, considering traductology and sociolinguistics as combative sport (as Pierre Bourdieu said when describing sociology).

Bibliography

Angoujard J-P., Manzano F., 2008, « Autour du gallo: état des lieux, analyses et perspectives », dans ANGOUJARD J-P., MANZANO F., (dirs.), *Autour du Gallo. Etat des lieux, analyses et perspectives*, Presses Universitaires de Rennes, Rennes, p. 5 to 10.

---

[30] Free translation of: « Une langue polynomique est une langue à l'unité abstraite, à laquelle les utilisateurs reconnaissent plusieurs modalités d'existence, toutes également tolérées sans qu'il y ait entre elles hiérarchisation ou spécialisation de fonction. Elle s'accompagne de l'intertolérance entre utilisateurs de variétés différentes sur les plans phonologiques et morphologiques, de même que la multiplicité lexicale est conçue ailleurs comme un élément de richesse » (Marcellesi J-B., 2003, (1989), 279).

Aufray R., 2007, Le petit Matao. Dictionnaire Gallo – Français. Motier Galo – Francçaez – Françaez – Galo, Rue des Scribes Editions, Rennes, 1004 pages.

Boghossian P., 2009, La peur du savoir. Sur le relativisme et le constructivisme de la connaissance, Agone, Marseille, 198 pages.

Boutet J., 2008, La vie verbale au travail. Des manufactures aux centres d'appels, Octares Editions, Toulouse, 202 pages.

Bouveresse J., 1997, *Dire et ne rien dire. L'illogisme, l'impossibilité et le nonsens*, Editions Jacqueline Chambon, Nîmes, 274 pages.

Breton R., 2003, *Atlas des langues du monde. Une pluralité fragile*, Editions Autrement, Paris, 82 pages.

Bulot T., 2006, La langue vivante. L'identité sociolinguistique des Cauchois, L'Harmattan, Paris, 226 pages.

Coulon A., 2002, *L'école de Chicago*, Presses Universitaires de France, Paris, 130 pages.

Eloy J-M., 2007, « La proximité des langues », dans Eloy J-M., Hifearnáin T., *Langues proches – langues collatérales. Near Languages – Collateral Languages*, L'Harmattan, Paris, p. 13 to 26.

Guidere M., 2010a, « L'Humanitaire face à la diversité ou la choc des perceptions », dans Guidere M. (dir.), *Traduction et médiation humanitaire*, Editions Le Manuscrit, Paris, p. 17 to 68.

Guidere M., 2010b, « Conclusion: l'intermédiation multilingue », dans Guidere M. (dir.), *Traduction et médiation humanitaire*, Editions Le Manuscrit, Paris, p. 205 to 209.

Jakobson R., 1963, « Aspects linguistiques de la traduction », dans Jakobson R., *Essais de linguistique générale. 1. Les fondations du langage*, Editions de Minuit, Paris, p. 78 to 86.

Lombard J., Vandewalle B., 2010, *Philosophie pour les professionnels de santé. Concepts et problématiques*, Editions Seli Arslan, Paris, 258 pages.

Manzano F., 2003, « Sur le contact français-gallo. Observations diachroniques, sociolinguistiques et anthropologiques », dans Leray C., Manzano F., (dirs), *Langues en contact. Canada, Bretagne*, Presses Universitaires de Rennes, Rennes, p. 133 to 177.

Marcellesi J-B., 2003, (1979), « Quelques problèmes de l'hégémonie culturelle en France: langue nationale et langues régionales », dans Marcellesi J-B. et Blanchet P., Bulot T., *Sociolinguistique. Epistémologie, Langues régionales, Polynomie*, L'Harmattan, Paris, p. 101 to 123.

Marcellesi J.-B., 2003, (1989), « Corse et théorie sociolinguistique: reflets croisés », dans Marcellesi J-B. et Blanchet P., Bulot T., *Sociolinguistique. Epistémologie, Langues régionales, Polynomie*, L'Harmattan, Paris, p. 273 to 282.

Ost F., 2009, Traduire. Défense et illustration du multilinguisme, Fayard, Paris, 434 pages.
Schleiermacher F., 1999, *Des différentes méthodes de traduire*, Seuil, Paris, 150 pages.
Searle J. R., 1998, *La construction de la réalité sociale*, Gallimard, Paris, 320 pages.
Snacken J., 1991, « Remarques préliminaires concernant l'"aide psycho-sociale dans une situation multiculturelle », dans GAILLY A., LEMAN J., (dirs.), *Thérapies interculturelles. L'interaction soignant-soigné dans un contexte multiculturel et interdisciplinaire*, De Boeck Université, Bruxelles, p. 7 to 10.
Wittgenstein L., 1965, Le cahier bleu et le cahier brun. Suivi de Ludwig Wittgenstein par Norman Malcolm, Gallimard, Paris, 436 pages.

Webography

Insee, 1999, « Langue bretonne et autres langues: pratique et transmission », on http://www.insee.fr/fr/insee_regions/bretagne/themes/octant/oc92/oc92art3.pdf, consulted in February, the 28th, 2011

Role and Value of Professional Translation in the European Union: A few leads on different scales

David Ar Rouz

The conference of which you are now reading the proceedings was held in Lorient, South Brittany (France). In this town, passers-by can notice many road signs like the following:

Image 1: Road signs of Lorient (photographs: © D. ar Rouz, 2010)

Some are bilingual French-Breton (e.g. "*UNIVERSITÉ de Bretagne-Sud / SKOL-VEUR Kreisteiz-Breizh*"), some are only in French ("*Présidence de l'U.B.S.*"), others bear Breton toponyms also used in French and need, therefore, no translation (*"LANVEUR / KERVENANEC"*), and the last kind of signs that are included here mixes bilingual designations and untranslated toponyms: "*LANVEUR – UNIVERSITÉ / SKOL-VEUR*".

This is because Lorient is located in the historical territory of the Breton language that extends in the western part of Brittany, from a linguistic border going approximately from the east of Vannes up to Saint-Brieuc. East of the border, people spoke Gallo, which, like French, is considered as an Oïl languages. Although these languages were widespread in the Breton countryside at the beginning of the twentieth century, Breton now counts only 206,000 speakers (Gaillard, 2009), that is 4.69% of the Breton population. Evaluating the number of Gallo speakers is more difficult, since speakers themselves do not often consider it a "language", but rather a form of distorted French. This explains that the INSEE survey found 28,300 speakers of Gallo in 1999 (Le Boëtté, 2003: 18), whereas a survey conducted by the CREDILIF research group estimated that they were rather between 200,000 and 400,000 (Chevalier, 2008), which represents between 0.64% and 9.11% of the Breton population.

As bilingual road signs can be considered the result of a translation process[1], as they are not, moreover, the only products of a professional translation service at work in Brittany, the region will provide an example on which some hypotheses about the role and value of professional translation are based here. The second example will be, as the title has announced, the European Union (EU).

Professional translation

Before analysing them, though, the meaning given to *professional translation* should be pointed out here, because, as Gagnepain said, "the least conversation is already a translation" (Gagnepain, 1994: 147, my translation). He explained the phenomenon by underlining that no one speaks exactly like one's interlocutor, no one understands exactly the same thing with the same words, because of different individual sociolinguistic histories. Conversation therefore needs, to some degree, an effort of translation that consists of two steps that have already been described for translation: the first one is the interpretation or hermeneutic phase (Ballard, 1993: 248), when one tries to grasp the meaning of what has been said or written; the second one is the *rewording* phase, as Jakobson put it when defining "intralingual translation"[2]. While the latter seems obvious in translation, it may not appear so in everyday conversation, for which two explanations can be provided:

- most of a conversation may be understood almost immediately, so that the rewording is not expressed, which does not mean that there is none;
- this rewording is in fact for oneself and the process happens most of the time unconsciously.

That is why it can only be supposed that it occurs all the time when something goes wrong in the exchange and then requires what Kerbrat-Orecchioni (1995: 194) called « les phénomènes de reprises » ("repetition phenomena"). They range from echolalia to questions through rewording, all aiming at checking that

---

1   We analysed this aspect of translation in depth in Ar Rouz & Le Squère, 2005.
2   Jakobson, « Aspects linguistiques de la traduction », *Essais de linguistique générale*, 1963, p. 79, quoted by Peeters, 1999: 16.

one has got the interlocutor's idea right. In some circumstances, especially when they are emotional, the founder of non-violent communication (NVC), Marshall B. Rosenberg, advises "paraphrasing" what has been said by the interlocutor (Rosenberg, 2003: 96-101), making then this phase of translation in conversation more visible.

Professional translation obviously has "something more" than everyday conversation, that one might call "*interpersonal translation*". It comes in when the sociolinguistic difference between interlocutors is too big for them to communicate effectively on their own. Then they need a third person whose responsibility it will be to enable their exchange by making mutual understanding possible. To do this, the translator (or interpreter) enters into a double interlocution (Peeters, 1999), with each of the people involved in the exchange: author and readers, for example, but also European Members of Parliament in Brussels, the town of Lorient and all the people going through the streets, be they speakers of Breton or not, etc.

The main characteristic of professional translation is that it takes place in a structured relationship of supply and demand. Not that both interlocutors should be engaged in a professional relationship, as diplomats may be, but both expect the translator to provide them the service they need for them to "converse" (and reading a book is a form of conversation as Peeters demonstrated[3]) or "communicate" when supplies and demands are prevailing in the exchange.

Translation demand

It might be said that the main demand from both interlocutors requiring a professional translator is mutual understanding. They want to be able to understand one another in order to have an exchange, with the possibility that the exchange itself may have other aims. In a number of situations, however, the exchange could be possible although people do not share the same mother tongue in the first place. This is exactly what happens in Brittany: all Bretons nowadays speak French, even Breton and Gallo speakers. So why is there professional translation into Breton? Another example would be the European Parliament: many members certainly speak foreign languages; they could, therefore, choose to communicate in a language common to all the interlocutors who are to work together.

---

3   See Peeters, 1999: 148-169.

In both cases, where self-translation[4] is possible, there is a language choice that leads to a request for professional translation. This is also how the historical example he gave in 2006 can be analysed:

> the use of an interpreter by the Irish Gaelic leader Hugh O'Neill in his dealings with Elizabeth I (even though he himself spoke English) was a way of initiating dialogue that nonetheless marked the cultural and political distance and difference between the two parties, thereby constructing interpreting as an activity of both interaction and resistance. (Cronin, 2006: 87)

Translation here is then a way to mark "cultural and political distance and difference". In the particular case of the Anglo-Irish conflict, it is easily understandable that an Irish Gaelic leader would choose to do so to represent his nation that he wants to remain independent.

Looking now to the perhaps more surprising example that we have mentioned: why would European Members of Parliament speak their own language if they can exchange with other members in a common language? One may indeed consider that they all belong to the same institution and that conflict should not be the main motivation of exchange, but a clear will to cooperate instead. One reason could be language loyalty: as elected representatives of their country in this supranational institution, members of Parliament should speak their national languages. Dollerup's explanation for this is the following:

> the politicians have not been elected for their ability to speak foreign languages, but in order to represent national voters; and in order to demonstrate to these very voters that they are doing their job, they must convey this information by speaking the national languages during debates – at least as long as the television cameras are on. (Dollerup, 2001: 274)

Once again, though, one might put forward the same need to mark "cultural and political distance and difference", because without it no negotiation would be possible:

> care for others, understanding of them, are only possible if one can adequately distinguish oneself from others. If I see myself as 'indistinct' from you, or you as not having your own being that is not merged with mine, then I cannot preserve a real sense of your well-being as opposed to mine. (Grimshaw, quoted by Cronin, 2003: 171)

When the Breton language is put forward, through publicly displayed translations[5], it serves as a distinctive mark of belonging as well. The translation department of the Breton Language Board, which has been public since September 2010 (Région Bretagne, 2010), explicitly states that they deal only with translations that will be public (Ofis ar Brezhoneg, 2003), with the exception of literature

---

[4] As Cronin understands it, that is translation of the self, or "translation-as-assimilation", as opposed to "auto-translation", translation of one's own writings and therefore "translation-as-diversification"(Cronin, 1998: 148, 158, published again in Cronin, 2003: 142, 154)

[5] See Ar Rouz & Le Squère (2005) for examples.

(Ofis ar Brezhoneg, 2006: 14). Such translations may be required for bilingual signing (on roadsides, in buildings such as hospitals, offices, supermarkets, factories, etc.), but the Board's works include other types of technical translation: software, websites, official forms, and so on. There is here another quite obvious reason for this language choice which requires translation: using the language in fields from which it had been excluded for decades is a means to develop its terminological resources. As Cronin put it:

> Language speakers can either be assimilated through self-translation to a dominant language or they can retain and develop their language through the good offices of translation and thus resist incorporation. (Cronin, 2003: 142)

The suggestion here is that, while this demand for translation seems obvious in the case of minority languages, it may also be a motive for translating in national languages, even at the European level. If Member States agreed to do with only one language in the European Union, what would become of their national languages? They would of course remain in use in their respective states, but they would have to wholly support the translation efforts regarding European terminology. Some may not be able to do it adequately and their languages would come to be more or less excluded from several fields dealt with by the EU. Another effect might be that speakers of these languages would try to learn and "self-translate" into the European language, progressively giving up their own. So, although to a lesser extent, development considerations are also important for European official languages and should not be forgotten in the debates about translation in all European languages.

Last but not least, a language choice may be made to enable speakers to think. The experience of "auto-translators" in this respect is quite interesting, as Julian Green explained:

> I laid aside what I had written [in French] and decided to begin the book again, this time in English, my intention being to use practically the same words, or, if you wish, to translate my own sentences into English.
>
> At this point something quite unexpected happened. With a very definite idea as to what I wanted to say I began my book, wrote about a page and a half and, on rereading what I had written, realized that I was writing another book, a book so different in tone from the French that a whole aspect of the subject must of necessity be altered. It was as if, writing in English, I had become another person. I went on. New trains of thoughts were started in my mind, new associations of ideas were formed. (Green, 1987: 174)

He simply tells us in this excerpt that a man thinks differently according to the language he is using. Thus, when people could speak another language than their own, yet choose to speak their own and resort to translation, the demand may be due to the fact that they want to think this way, to feel comfortable in the process of thinking and sharing their thought.

Translation in the European Union

The European Union has done with twenty-three official languages since 2007. No other international organisation has so many: the United Nations Organisation, with 192 member states, has only six official languages. No wonder then that the EU would rely upon the largest translation services in the world. The following image gives an overview of these services and the translating staff:

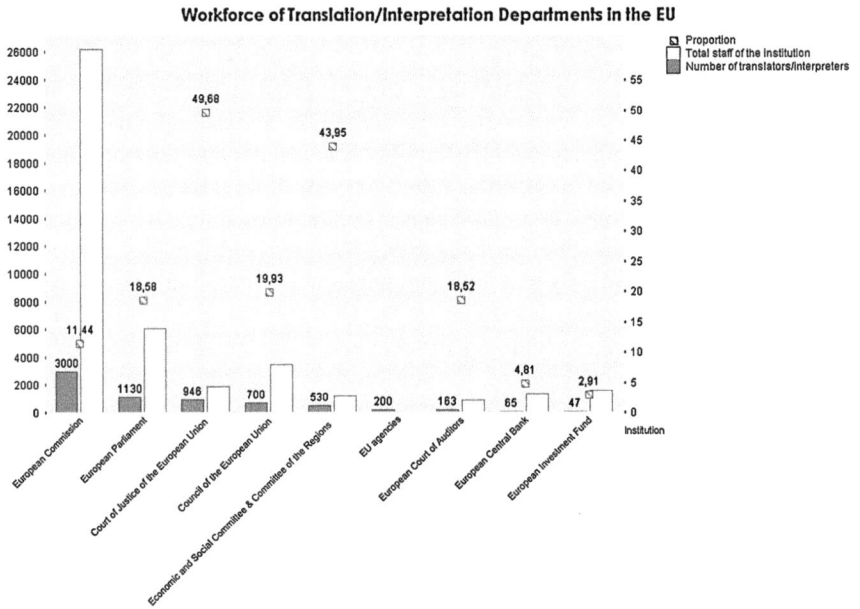

Image 2:   Workforce of Translation/Interpretation Departments in the EU (© D. ar Rouz, 2011)

According to the numbers that could be gathered from different sources to build this graphic[6], the total number of translators and interpreters in the EU would amount to 6,781 out of a total staff of 76,973, which represents 8.81%.

Translation is, however, organised in many different ways. Firstly, the European law, and in particular Regulation No. 1 of 1958, distinguishes two main language systems. It mentions the external system, on the one hand, which has to do with the relationships between the institutions and the Member States and citizens in

---

6   They are the websites of the institutions, Rinsche et al., (2009: 36), Pariente (2010: 49), and the establishment plan staff (http://eur-lex.europa.eu/LexUriServ/LexUriServ.do?uri=OJ:L:2010:064:0001:01:EN:HTML).

any of the official languages (Art. 2 & 3), but also with the publications of the Union: "Regulations and other documents of general application shall be drafted in the official languages." (Art. 4), "The Official Journal of the Community shall be published in the official languages." (Art. 5); and the internal one, on the other hand: "The institutions of the Community may stipulate in their rules of procedure which of the languages are to be used in specific cases." (Art. 6). Hence, there are a number of different internal systems which, in turn, imply different organisations of the translation services. To take only two examples, the European Commission adopted three procedural languages (English, French and German), whereas the Court of Justice deliberates in French.

Secondly, the services are also organised according to the needs identified in each institution which depend themselves on the role of the institution in the Union. Thus, the European Commission, which is in charge of producing most of the legislative texts to be discussed, voted and published for the Union, comprises the biggest number of translators (2,500), with a smaller number of interpreters (500) who represent 16.67% of the total translating staff. The needs in the Commission could be the internal needs of the Commissioners in the procedural languages or, in all official languages: contact with Member States, companies or citizens, production of "Regulations and other documents of general application", etc.

In comparison, the European Parliament, the main task of which could be said to consist in organising debates between its members, employs 430 in-house interpreters against "only" 700 translators (interpreters represent then 38.05% of the translating staff), but "has at its disposal a reserve of some 2500 freelance interpreters"[7] and specifies that up to

> Between 800 and 1000 interpreters are on hand for the plenary sittings of Parliament, at which simultaneous interpretation is provided from and into all the EU's official languages.[7]

Although they could be considered "internal" as they involve the Members of Parliament and other staff from other institutions, plenary sittings are also public, would it be only because of the publication of the report of proceedings, even in the form of videos on the website of the Parliament. This, together with the need for every representative who can be elected without any particular language skill, explains that plenary sittings should occur in the twenty-three official languages. On the contrary, for other meetings between Members of Parliament, in committees, political groups or others, where the number of participants is reduced, interpretation provision is organised according to the (internal) needs expressed by the participants.

---

7   Website of the European Parliament: http://www.europarl.europa.eu/parliament/public/static Display.do?language=EN&refreshCache=yes&pageRank=4&id=155, consulted on 1st March 2011.

By studying more thoroughly the organisation of the services and the changes in it over time – which is especially relevant and feasible for the largest service, the Directorate-General for Translation (DGT), because their history was published in 2010 (Pariente, 2010) –, it can be clearly seen that translation offers in the European Union have been adapting themselves to the growing demand, especially since the preparation of the biggest enlargement ever in 2004. For example, the DGT has been offering since 2006 a service of "linguistic and stylistic revision of English and French originals" (Pariente, 2010: 50) or a "Web" unit to translate the contents of the Europa websites.

In any case, the basic roles of translation in the European Union may be reduced to two propositions:

1. Professional translation certainly enables interlocutions and understanding between people that would not be able to exchange otherwise.
2. It also enables language choice, even though a common language may be found between the interlocutors.

Suggestions have already been made about why people might choose their own language in such situations, but the analysis of the value of professional translation can still be extended by giving some elements of its cost and being more specific about its benefits.

The Costs of Translation

One cannot but be stricken, when reading books about linguistic policies, by the place given – or rather refused – to translation. Calvet, for example, does not mention it when listing the means that people use to overcome their linguistic differences (Calvet, 2002: 17). But in this book and in a previous one (1996)[8], he commented extensively on the costs of translation, which could be classified into three categories.

The first most obvious one is the *financial cost* of maintaining such services in the European Union. Calvet considers that "the majority of European civil servants work in language services, even though 0.8% of the total budget may seem less than 40% of the operating budget..." (Calvet, 2002: 44, my translation)[9]. We have shown that translators and interpreters were very far from constituting the majority of European civil servants. The issue of the budget and oper-

---

8   See in particular Calvet, 1996: 101 and Calvet, 2002: 43-50, 100, 135-137, 192-194.
9   "La majorité des fonctionnaires européens travaille dans les services linguistiques, même si 0,8 % du budget total peuvent paraître moins importants que 40 % du budget de fonctionnement ..."

ating budget could be investigated further, but the fact is that, contrary to Grin's expectations before the 2004 enlargement (Grin, 2004: 5), the cost of translation has remained about two euros per year and head of population:

> The second myth is that a huge proportion of the budget of the European Union is spent on multilingualism, whereas the costs of translation and interpretation in all the EU institutions account for less than 1% of the total annual budget of the European Union (corresponding to approximately €2 per head of population). (Pariente, 2010: 56)

Of course, this is not the only element of cost that Calvet points out. He mentions the difficulty of finding interpreters for some language combinations too, mainly to emphasize that interpretation occurs then through pivot languages ('relay' interpreting) and implies therefore still more *semantic losses*. From the point of view of translation studies, this hypothesis may be questioned and this is what Dollerup did:

> In my experience 'relay' does not lead to the number of errors in the interpreting at the EU that many would believe. The reason is that EU interpreters are top professionals.[10] Errors do occur in interpreting, but the vast majority are due to delegates who throw in slang, names, come up with complicated figures, speak dialects, hit microphones, etc. On the other hand, relay is a major management problem. (Dollerup, 2001: 279)

He stresses then that the problems relate more to time-lag in communication and staff management. Semantic losses may indeed happen in translation, but the question that can be asked is: are there more of them in translation than in any monolingual conversation? Moreover, considering that translation through pivot languages entails only semantic losses leads one to ignore the idea that the process may sometimes improve the clarity of the original message.

The same difficulty of recruitment manifests another element of cost that he refers to as "*administrative red tape*". There is little doubt that any translation requires more time than a simple conversation, would it be only because it demands that the translator enter into two successive interlocutions. Even in the so-called "simultaneous" interpreting, there is a short time lag, only a few seconds, between the moment the hearer sharing the same language as the speaker grasps the meaning of what he is saying and the moment a hearer expecting interpretation can understand it too. The administrative red tape is particularly clear when one studies the issue of deadlines. In 1954, a complex process is set up and the

---

10 I discuss the problems in relay interpreting in some detail in Dollerup 1996. There are several factors at work, but the most important is the professionalism of the interpreters at international organisations. The presence of both sender and recipients as well as body language, and, finally, the minutes from meetings all contribute to a minimum of errors at meetings. There is thus nothing contradictory in that Susan Šarčević (below, p. xx) points out that translators working with written material and who do not have access to similar correctives, should be wary of relay. (The author's endnote)

reference deadline is then of 48 hours for priority documents and 52 hours for more important documents, extra time being negotiated for particular documents (Vieilledent-Monfort, 2009: 17). In 2004, the Parliament set a "tabling deadline"[11] of ten days, which the Council had also done in 1998 (Court of Auditors, 2006: 14). The same report indicates, however, that "these deadlines are rarely observed" and that "DGT's planning unit regularly renegotiates deadlines".

Deadlines are not the only constraint imposed on users of the translation services. The Court of Auditors's report thus explains that they

> are required by the translation services to indicate references to existing similar translated documents and/or to show changes made to the previous version of a document already translated. (*Ibid.*)

The length of documents has been another recurrent issue since 1954 in the Commission, which decided, for example, in 2004 to "reduce the length of documents intended for the College of Commissioners to not more than fifteen pages" (Pariente, 2010: 46), but it is also limited by other institutions (Court of Auditors, 2006). In the same way, when "late changes to originals" are identified as a problem for translation and translation costs at the beginning of 2000 (Pariente, 2010: 40), it is decided to have most documents translated only when they are considered "stable".

Calvet says that:

> the defence of "smaller" languages, as it is expressed in the Universal Declaration of Linguistic Rights or in the European Charter for Regional and Minority Languages, and in the "politico-linguistically correct" speech in general, would be the manifestation of a luxury accessible at a certain time in the history of developed countries that has little to do with the problems of developing countries which, in any case, cannot afford it. (Calvet, 2002: 174, my translation)[12]

As has been seen, there may not be more difference between the demand of translation into Breton and the demand of translation in the official languages of the European Union than one of degree. Given Calvet's comments about translation in the EU, it could be extrapolated and asserted that for him, as well as for many other people, translation itself is considered a luxury. However, despite the considerations which have been brought forward here on the costs of translation, it should not be assumed that the same above conclusions of professional transla-

---

11 "A tabling deadline is the minimum incompressible time allocated to a translation service to issue a requested translation." (Court of Auditors, 2006: 14)

12 La défense des « petites » langues, telle qu'elle se manifeste dans la Déclaration universelle des droits linguistiques ou dans la Charte européenne des langues, et de façon plus générale dans le discours PLC, serait la manifestation d'un luxe accessible en un moment de l'histoire des pays développés n'ayant que peu de liens avec les problèmes des pays en voie de développement qui, de toute façon, ne peuvent pas s'offrir ce luxe.

tion being a luxury are to be drawn, as all the benefits that it carries with it have not yet been taken into account.

The Benefits of Translation

The previously mentioned constraints at the EU level all aim at enabling the translation services to keep on dealing as efficiently as possible with a growing demand and at "rationalising resources" (Pariente, 2010: 40). The whole history of translation at the European Commission is quite telling of the growing awareness of the importance of translation. The Translation Service became indeed independent, headed by a Director-General, in 1989, before becoming a Directorate-General of its own in 2002 (*ibid.*: 30, 42). It was also given the possibility by this time to "give its opinion in the "interservice consultation" process" (*ibid.*: 40), the "procedure in the course of which a number of Commission departments express their opinion on a particular subject" (*ibid.*: 74), which can be the drafting of laws. As seen here, however, costs are sometimes more easily seen that benefits and it may now be useful to outline a few of them.

In a conference about science and Arabic held in Cairo in 2003, Calvet studied how translations to Arabic enabled the progress of Arabic science, and translations from Arabic then allowed its diffusion in the world. In the publication of this work in 2007, he asserted that "only a translation policy, included in larger linguistic policies, can guarantee the progress of science" (Calvet, 2007: 51). Peeters, in a conference delivered in Lorient on 1st March 2011[13], explained the same idea that translation and translators contributed throughout history to the *elaboration of knowledge and science*.

In the contemporary contexts of the European Union and Brittany, translations are obviously not mainly directed towards science. As stated, the first benefit of translation in such political frameworks is the nature of the process itself, its social role, which consists in *enabling interlocution between people who do not share a common language*. But the case of Brittany first, where all inhabitants are supposed to share French and translations into Breton are nevertheless publicly displayed, suggests that the benefit of translation may also lie in a *recognition of difference*.

It was then noted that, although the official languages of the European Union are not "minority languages", the same might be true at this supranational level. Thanks to translation, people within the organisation can choose to use their own language, different as it may be from their interlocutor's. In the EU, this is con-

---

13 The video will be accessible online at: http://www.univ-ubs.fr/mdr/mardis/audiovisuel.htm.

sidered a fundamental right of individuals: being able to understand the information provided by the EU, to communicate with institutions, to be elected as a representative of their country without any particular language skill, etc.:

> At the Commission, the annual costs for translation are estimated at €300 million – which is equivalent to about €0.60 per head of population per year and a modest price to pay for guaranteeing *democracy and equal rights among citizens.* (Pariente, 2010: 56, my emphasis)

It is precisely because this important cultural difference is recognised that people (members of Parliament, civil servants, citizens) may engage in fruitful cooperation. Pym based his reflection on an ethics of translation on the idea that translation should be used "*to ease cooperation*" (Pym, 1997: 13, my translation). As Gagnepain said: "We negotiate only because we have established borders" (Gagnepain, 1994: 42, my translation). Thus, just as it highlights the linguistic and cultural border that separates people, professional translation constitutes certainly an excellent means to overcome it.

Another way in which professional translation does this is by enabling the negotiators to choose the language in which they feel best. The point here is not so much negotiation in itself, at the social level, as the relationship of each person to language and to himself or herself. In non-violent communication (NVC), Rosenberg stressed the necessity of such a connection to oneself: "When we are connected to our need, whether it is for reassurance, purposefulness, or solitude, we are in touch with our life energy." (Rosenberg, 2003: 143) To communicate effectively, he suggests then indeed the use of a four-step process consisting in formulating 1) observations on what has happened; 2) feelings or emotions triggered by events or exchanges; 3) basic needs that one's feelings "translate" as satisfied or not in the relationship. The fourth and last step of the process is a request consisting in a suggestion of a concrete and negotiable action.

Authors and non-violent communication workshop organisers feel the need to provide their readers and participants with long lists of words expressing basic needs (*ibid.*: 54-55), and feelings when needs are being met or not (*ibid.*: 44-46), because they see that the lack of vocabulary prevents people from engaging into the process of non-violent communication: they do not get their feelings and needs right, are subsequently unable to express them accurately to others and go back to violent expressions of their needs. In such lists, even if all words may be known, at least by native speakers, most of them are probably never used.

This is another benefit that interlocutors may draw from choosing, thanks to professional translation, their own language in order to engage into a communication process: they would *a priori* have the largest vocabulary regarding how they feel and what they need, which is the basis for non-violent communication. In other words, professional translation would give people involved in an exchange *the best chances to remain affectively connected to themselves and therefore to others*.

Translation that appears too often as an additional cost hindering direct communication between individuals—or that is suspected of distortion and even treachery—is actually the essential price to pay, to which everyone of us should give consent, to establish a feeling of identity and language security favourable to peace and the building of the knowledge society. (Yannic, 2010: 32-33, my translation)[14]

Non-violent communication is precisely based on an inner sense of security, not only related to language but to one's value at large as a human being, and it can be felt only if one remains connected to him/herself in the exchange. This connection often goes through a process of *"intrapersonal translation"* in which sensations and feelings are interpreted; words are then needed to complete the process and *name* them adequately. This is where, in my opinion, professional translation comes in.

Not so far from the ideas of non-violent communication, James Redfield offers, in a series of novels and books[15], a more extensive vision of human relationships and history. He explains indeed that, in the Middle Ages, Churches lost their power on existential questions. People then looked for answers in science, but the answers that were suggested did not prove quite satisfactory, still less unshakable. Material aspects of life (economics) became an obsession, but now that material comfort has been reached, the feeling that there must be "something else" to life seems more and more widespread. He argues that a new spiritual awareness of a responsive, "energy-dynamic universe" can be felt, thus leading more and more people to try to connect directly to the divine energy around them instead of engaging in control dramas and manipulations destined to get energy from other people.

The question that Redfield's vision raises here is the following: does this vision apply to European history? In a broad outline, it could be said that after centuries of wars that tore apart the European continent, which is also a way to get "energy" from others, a few people imagined that previously enemy States could work together to rebuild their economies. They created the European Coal and Steel Community (ECSC) in 1951, then the European Economic Community (EEC) and Euratom in 1957, before merging these institutions to create the European Union in 1992. By this time, even if economies of the partner countries may not always have been flourishing, they have at least allowed most of their

---

14 La traduction qui apparaît trop souvent comme un coût supplémentaire et une entrave à la communication directe entre les individus – ou que l'on suspecte de déformation et même de « trahison » – est en réalité le prix indispensable, auquel chacun de nous doit consentir, pour que s'instaure un sentiment de sécurité identitaire et linguistique propice à la paix et à l'instauration de la société de la connaissance.

15 See for example the initial novel titled *The Celestine Prophecy* (1993), or *The Celestine Vision* (1998), where he explains how he came to write the books and what his vision is.

inhabitants to have a comfortable standard of living. Material security having been reached, it was time to launch the political construction of Europe which is still going on nowadays.

Is it surprising, in this context, that professional translation has gained importance? Can it be only by chance that translation, along with culture and cultural diversity, comes right to the fore in a period of history when more than economic cooperation is sought? In this view, translation would appear still less as a luxury, rather as an invaluable step in history towards peace. Perhaps not so much because "the effect of this global conversation is to make our interpretation of words and phrases, even across various languages, much more accurate" (Redfield, 1998: 141), as because translation is, on the contrary, a negotiation across borders that have previously been recognised and welcomed.

Redfield's vision may be considered too occidental, for it seems obvious that the standard of living in developed countries cannot be compared to that of developing countries. Yet, he also highlights the attraction exerted by Eastern philosophies (*ibid.*: 55-57) in the West, for example, which gives an insight into a form of intercultural dialogue that would be profitable to all countries. Furthermore, if the value of translation is considered according to its outline here, with highly valuable – although not commercial at all – benefits, it could be argued that professional translation could be set up as a true policy in developing countries too, in order to foster another kind of cooperation and development, less centred on material comfort than on human well-being.

For a comprehensive analysis of translation value

Such a view of translation benefits, which takes into account human relationships, can bring significant changes to the analysis of translation value. For this analysis to be comprehensive, however, the economic aspects of both costs and benefits should not be forgotten. As Grin advocates, the study of costs and benefits should include moreover what he calls "transfers" (Grin, 2004: 3). In 2004, he conducted a comparison of six different language systems that could be chosen for the European Union:

- monarchistic: English (or another language belonging to one or several States in the EU) as the only official language;
- synarchic: Esperanto (or another third language, like Latin) as the only official language;
- oligarchic: a few official languages only;
- panarchic: all languages official, the system currently in use;

- hegemonic: all languages official but one of them as pivot language;
- technocratic: all languages official but Esperanto (e.g.) as pivot language.

He showed very well that none was the absolute best: it depends on the chosen criteria. He also gave examples of indirect elements of both financial and social costs for the community (that may be seen as benefits by some in the community): if the monarchistic system was chosen and the language selected was English, publishers in the British Isles would benefit from an immense market for pedagogical tools; native English speakers would need no translation, no editing, no language learning and the English-speaking states could invest the corresponding savings in other fields in which they would become more competitive; non natives would be at a disadvantage in the exchanges; etc.

It could also be forwarded that a comprehensive analysis of translation value in the European Union should consider what could replace the current system. However, it should be first pointed out that such a change cannot be decided without having pondered the actual value of the panarchic system, compared perhaps to other budget lines; secondly, that it may help to consider flexible systems instead of rigid ones.

Grin (2004: 9) finds that the use of Esperanto could be a "key element" for a long-term solution in the EU, especially in a technocratic language system. But why, for example, should *one* pivot language be agreed upon? Need it be controlled? In 2003, a report already indicated that the European Parliament had generalised the use of three pivot languages: English, French and German (Herbillon, 2003). Couldn't it be imagined that translators and interpreters would resort to the pivot language of their choice, according to their language skills? This would avoid massive "transfers" compared to only one imposed pivot language. Another question regarding an official pivot language: wouldn't it entail additional costs, since any translation would imply two translations instead of only one today? Or perhaps costs would only be "transferred": fewer translators but more translations.

Further questions arise too concerning the artificial nature of Esperanto. If people feel "weakened" (Grin, 2004: 6) in the exchange when they must use a foreign language, what would happen with Esperanto, that would have to be learnt by all, translators and interpreters included? Even though it may be easier and cheaper to learn than any other language, it cannot be considered beforehand that all will dedicate the same time and resources to the task, especially because they would have no affective urge to do so, as Urien highlighted about the need to learn Breton (Urien, 1989: 37). Equality in this respect may be pure illusion.

It would be equally misleading to imagine that the use of only one pivot language would reduce terminology discrepancies, mistakes and misunderstandings, simply because they are constitutive of social verbal exchanges and cultural differences, which would express themselves in other ways within the common language. So, one may agree with the method that Grin uses to analyse the value of translation, and his work should certainly be given a significant place in any analysis of this kind, but one should not agree with his conclusion before other elements and possibilities have been explored.

Conclusion

In the present article, the intent was to show first that situations like the Breton one may help us understand why professional translation is needed. Such a situation allows one to see more than the common belief that translation serves only to connect people, beyond the border of different languages. In fact, the very condition of its capacity to connect people might well lie in how it makes diversity acknowledged for interlocutors. Then, they can engage in cooperation and negotiation.

That is why the value of professional translation goes far beyond financial considerations. After reminding some elements of translation cost (expenses, losses in communication, administrative red tape), I mentioned considerable benefits. A look back in the history of translation reveals its role in the elaboration of knowledge and science. The political frameworks considered, however, reveal other dimensions. Apart from the communication it enables between people who do not share the same language, precisely by recognising their differences, translation is thus an instrument of democracy thanks to which people can choose their preferred language. This choice, in turn, gives them the best possibilities to remain connected to their own selves, by what was called here "intrapersonal translation". References to the non-violent communication method provided a new insight into this invaluable benefit of translation.

Reference was also made to Redfield's vision, providing the understanding that translation at this point in European history may correspond to a more and more widespread quest for "intrapersonal" translation, spirituality, energy and connection with other human beings. With so many elements on the benefit side of this analysis of translation value, it can doubtfully still be considered "a luxury". The EU example shows in this respect that a translation policy can effectively serve to accommodate linguistic and cultural diversity, keeping expenses to a reasonable amount of less than 1% of the total budget. It can certainly be improved, and this is what the DGT, in particular, has been doing for decades. It should not be forgotten, nevertheless, that improvement depends on the dominant criteria at one point in time and that these criteria are based similarly on an analysis of value as a relationship between costs and benefits. Hence the interest of conducting further research about the social and axiological elements of translation value.

Bibliography

Ansembourg Thomas (d'). Cessez d'être gentil soyez vrai. Être avec les autres en restant soi-même. Montreal: Les Éditions de l'Homme, 2004.

Ar Rouz (Le Roux) David. « Compte rendu ». *Comment l'Europe 'parle' aux citoyens: un défi linguistique.* Brussels: DLF Bruxelles-Europe, 2010. http://www.langue-francaise.org/Bruxelles/Multi_28_09_2010_compte_rendu.pdf.

Ar Rouz (Le Roux) David. « Le traducteur: équilibriste des frontières ». in: PEETERS Jean (sous la direction de). *Traduction et communautés.* Arras: Artois Presses Université, 2010.

Ar Rouz (Le Roux) David. « Le breton à la conquête de la modernité ». in: Nadiani Giovanni, Giorgio Marrano Michela & Rundle Chris (editors). *The Translation of Dialects in Multimedia. inTRAlinea Online Translation Journal,* Special Issue. Forlì: Université de Bologne, 2009. http://www.intralinea.it.

Ar Rouz (Le Roux) David & Le Squère Roseline. « Traduction et affichage public: quel(s) service(s) pour les langues régionales de Bretagne? ». in: Moïse Claudine, Fillol Véronique et Bulot Thierry. *Langues régionales. Marges linguistiques,* No 10. November. Saint-Chamas: M.L.M.S. Éditeur, 2005. p. 190-206.

Ballard Michel (sous la direction de). *La traduction à l'université. Recherches et propositions didactiques.* Lille: Presses Universitaires de Lille, 1993.

Calvet Louis-Jean. « La mondialisation au filtre des traductions ». in: Nowicki Joanna & Oustinoff Michaël. *Traduction et mondialisation, volume 1. Hermès,* No 49. Paris: CNRS Éditions, 2007. p. 45-57.

Calvet Louis-Jean. Le marché aux langues. Essai de politologie linguistique sur la mondialisation. Paris: Plon, 2002.

Chevalier Gwendal. « Gallo et breton: complémentarité ou concurrence? ». in: Angoujard J.P. & Manzano Francis. *Autour du gallo: état des lieux, analyses et perspectives. Cahiers de Sociolinguistique,* No 12. Rennes: Presses Universitaires de Rennes (P.U.R.), 2008. p. 75-109.

Court of Auditors. "Special Report No 9/2006 concerning translation expenditure incurred by the Commission, the Parliament and the Council together with the Institutions' replies". *Official Journal of the European Union,* C 284.

2006. p. 1-39. http://www.eur-lex.europa.eu/LexUriServ/LexUriServ.do?uri= OJ:C:2006:284:0001:0039:EN:PDF. Downloaded on 2nd March 2011.

Cronin Michael. *Translation and Identity.* Oxon: Routledge, 2006.

Cronin Michael. *Translation and Globalization.* Oxon: Routledge, 2003.

Dollerup Cay. "Complexities of EU Language Work". *Perspectives: Studies in Translatogy,* volume 9 issue 4. 2001. p. 271-292. http://cay-dollerup.dk/Docs/181%20Complexities%20of%20EU%20translation%20work%202002%20-%20181.doc. Téléchargé le 16 mars 2011.

Gagnepain Jean. Leçons d'introduction à la Théorie de la Médiation. Anthropologiques, 5. Louvain-la-Neuve: Peeters, 1994.

Gaillard Philippe. « Moins de 200 000 personnes parlent le breton ». *Ouest France,* No 19618. 11th March 2009. p. 7.

Green Julien. Le langage et son double / The Language and its Shadow. Paris: Éditions du Seuil, 1987.

Grin François. « Coûts et justice linguistique dans l'élargissement de l'Union européenne ». in: Favre D'echallens Marc. *L'avenir s'écrit aussi en français. Panoramiques,* No 69. 4th quarter 2004. p. 97-104. Downloaded on 14th June 2010.

Herbillon Michel. *Rapport d'information sur la diversité linguistique dans l'Union européenne.* No 902. 11 June. Paris: Assemblée nationale, 2003. http://www.assemblee-nationale.fr/12/europe/rap-info/i0902.asp#TopOfPage. Downloaded on 26 November 2010.

Kerbrat-Orecchioni Catherine. *Les interactions verbales.* Tome I. Paris: Armand Colin, 1995. 1st published in 1990. Coll. « Linguistique ».

Le Boëtté Isabelle. « Langue bretonne et autres langues: pratique et transmission ». *Octant,* No 92. January 2003. p. 18-22. http://www.insee.fr/fr/insee_regions/bretagne/themes/octant/oc92/oc92art3.pdf. Downloaded on 9th February 2010.

Ofis Ar Brezhoneg / Office de la Langue Bretonne. *Rapport d'activité 2005.* Rennes: 2006. Downloaded on 2nd July 2006.

Ofis Ar Brezhoneg / Office de la Langue Bretonne. *Conditions et tarifs 2003 du service de traduction.* 2003.

Oustinoff Michaël, Nowicki Joanna & Machado da Silva Juremir. *Traduction et mondialisation, volume 2. Hermès,* No 56. Paris: CNRS Éditions, 2010.

Pariente Audrey. *Translation at the European Commission – a history.* Luxembourg: Office for Official Publications of the European Communities, 2010.

Peeters Jean. La médiation de l'étranger. Une sociolinguistique de la traduction. Arras: Artois Presses Université, 1999.

Pym Anthony. *Pour une éthique du traducteur.* Arras: Artois Presses Université, 1997. Collection « Traductologie ».

Redfield James. *The Celestine Vision. Living the New Spiritual Awareness.* Reading: Bantam Books, 1998. (1st published in 1997).

Redfield James. *La prophétie des Andes.* Traduit de l'américain par Bernard Willerval. Paris: Éditions J'ai Lu, 1996. (1st published in 1994). Collection « Aventure secrète ».

Région Bretagne. « Un nouvel Etablissement public de coopération culturelle pour la langue bretonne ». 2010. http://www.bretagne.fr/internet/jcms/pre prod_86387/un-nouvel-etablissement-public-de-cooperation-culturelle-pour-la-langue-bretonne. Consulted on 17th October 2010.

Rinsche Adriane & Portera-Zanotti Nadia. *Study on the size of the language industry in the EU.* Luxembourg: European Commission, 2009.

Rosenberg Marshall B. *Nonviolent Communication. A Language of Life.* Encinitas: PuddleDancer Press, 2003. 2nd Edition.

Urien Jean-Yves. La trame d'une langue: le breton. Présentation d'une théorie de la syntaxe et application. Lesneven: Mouladurioù Hor Yezh, 1989.

Vieilledent-Monfort Catherine. *Études sur la traduction et le multilinguisme. La traduction à la Commission: 1958-2010.* Bruxelles: Commission européenne, 2009. http://ec.europa.eu/dgs/translation/publications/index_fr.htm. Downloaded on 1st September 2010.

Yannic Aurélien. « Francophonie, plurilinguisme, traduction: la mondialisation des enjeux identitaires ». in: Oustinoff Michaël, Nowicki Joanna & Machado da Silva Juremir. *Traduction et mondialisation, volume 2. Hermès,* No 56. Paris: CNRS Éditions, 2010. p. 29-34.

Dissémination et triangle culturel: réalités orientales dans deux romans « algériens » contemporains de langue française

Mirela Kumbaro-Furxhi and Yves Gambier

1. Mise en perspective et problématique

Entre l'étrangeté du texte de départ et la lisibilité du texte d'arrivée, il y a le travail du traducteur. Etrangeté et lisibilité sont deux notions complexes et relatives qui sont fonction du récepteur, et dans ce cas en premier lieu du traducteur, lecteur prototypique des lecteurs à venir.

Nos exemples de comparaison vont porter sur *Le festin de mensonges* d'Amin Zaoui (2007), traduit en albanais (2008), et *La Goutte d'Or* de Michel Tournier (1986), traduit en suédois (1987). Ces deux romans « algériens », écrits en français, situés dans un contexte arabe maghrébin contemporain (années 1960-1980), sont comme des récits initiatiques dans le sens où les principaux protagonistes, adolescents, se dépouillent peu à peu de certaines représentations de soi pour se découvrir une certaine identité. L'un le fait en levant divers tabous érotiques et religieux à travers des expériences intimes, l'autre à la suite du parcours physique de l'émigration, depuis son oasis natal dans le Sahara jusqu'au quartier éponyme de Paris.

Si les deux romans proposent une vision de l'homme et du monde, c'est grâce à une structure narrative bien différente. Dans *Le festin*, le « je » est la voix dominante, ponctuée de rappels – de l'indépendance à la Guerre des six jours. Le narrateur se met en scène dans la co-présence de musulmans et de juifs, entre fantasmes et actualités. Dans *La Goutte d'Or*, le point de vue est extérieur: Idriss est (mal)mené à travers des réalités (désert, mariage rituel, voyage, métiers, abattoir, etc.) et des images (photos, publicités, affiches, miroir, mannequins), maitrisées par l'auteur. L'ensemble des brefs chapitres est ponctué par deux récits allégoriques, légendaires (sur le portrait du roi et la reine blonde) et un postscriptum où Tournier laisse croire à la dimension documentaire de son travail romanesque.

Les chaines de références intertextuelles, les allusions diffèrent aussi d'une oeuvre à l'autre. Si Zaoui met son texte en résonance avec Flaubert, Baudelaire, des citations du Coran et des faits d'actualité (le pensionnat, les Frères musulmans, la guerre éclair de 1967, etc.), Tournier se propose une réflexion sur les pouvoirs plutôt maléfiques de l'image et l'image des pouvoirs (de la femme, de la mère, de l'oncle, des patrons) – Idriss ne se reconnaissant pas dans ce que lui renvoie l'autre. Ce qui n'exclut pas des références à des poèmes, à des écrivains, à des chansons, etc.

Ces différences n'entravent pas notre objectif, à savoir comment les traducteurs rendent la toile complexe des non-dits, de l'implicite, des présupposés, des associations, des correspondances des originaux. Comment les représentations du monde arabo-musulman se transforment – elles dans des textes directement écrits (« traduits ») en français quand ces textes « retournent » à leur source musulmane (le livre de Zaoui, publié en France et censuré en Algérie, s'adresse quand il est traduit en albanais à un lecteur plutôt de tradition musulmane) ou quand ces textes « se déplacent » dans un autre contexte (le livre de Tournier partage le même code culturel et le même imaginaire que ses lecteurs francophones, tout en déconstruisant un certain « exotisme », mais perd cette complicité quand il est traduit en suédois, les nouveaux lecteurs n'ayant pas le même héritage colonial, la même familiarité avec les repères et éléments culturels, les clichés manichéens comme par exemple blonde/brune, mère/prostituée, du texte de départ)?

Ce « retour » et ce « décentrement », nous allons les subsumer par la notion de « triangle culturel ». Nous proposons nos deux analyses, sans recours aux comptes rendus critiques (journalistiques – accueil plutôt mitigé de *La Goutte d'Or*) ni aux recherches universitaires (assez nombreuses concernant Tournier), selon nos perspectives propres: d'abord sur le mode du « je » par la traductrice de Zaoui puis sur le mode du « il » par le lecteur de Tournier.

2. Périple traductionnel du Festin de mensonges

Lors de la traduction du livre *Festin de mensonges,* j'ai essayé de donner une forme et un nom au périple traductionnel que j'ai connu lors de ce travail qui a vu le jour sous sa forme albanaise en 2008.

Amin Zaoui y relate les années de formation de Koussalaï, son jeune héros. L'action se déroule dans les années 1960, plus précisément, du 19 juin 1965, jour du putsch de Houari Boumediene contre Ben Bella, à la guerre des Six-Jours, en juin 1967, deux dates clefs, selon l'auteur, annonciatrices de haine et de mort. Le jeune personnage est partagé entre les contraintes morales de la religion et l'appel pressant des plaisirs interdits. Il se soustrait peu à peu à l'obsession du péché en découvrant la « religion véridique », celle des libres penseurs des siècles d'or de l'islam. *Festin de mensonges n*'est pas pour autant un roman anti-religieux, le narrateur adolescent ne déclare la guerre ni à Dieu ni à ses apôtres. C'est un voyage initiatique pour l'enfant dans le monde des sens, alors qu'est dépeint la montée des plus importants courants de la géopolitique arabe: glorification du panarabisme, suite à la défaite arabe contre Israël. Le protagoniste assiste spectateur aux plus grandes mutations de l'histoire de son pays. À l'image d'une société algérienne qui se cherche, « ... notre histoire est composée de défaites, de manipulations, de tromperies et de pleurs », dit-il. Un miroir, qui met à nu une certaine culture du non-dit.

Comédie de mœurs, *Festin de Mensonges* dresse un tableau sans complaisance des maux et travers de la société arabe et musulmane où tout se fait dans l'intolérance et le secret. Ce roman se construit autour de la transgression de ce qui peut être appelé le «triple tabou arabe»: le sexe, la religion et la politique. Il n'est pas étonnant que le livre de cet auteur, ancien directeur de la Bibliothèque Nationale d'Alger, limogé car il dérangeait, soit censuré en Algérie et que Fayard le reçoive en France. C'est une littérature qui m'a appelé non pas par son exotisme, mais par le courage d'aborder l'interdit, la critique par l'humour et par ses trouvailles littéraires. Ce sont des éléments qui ne peuvent pas laisser indifférente la traductrice d'un pays qui a connu les tabous, les interdits et les manipulations idéologiques au service d'une dictature.

L'éditeur m'a proposé le livre pour s'en faire une opinion: j'ai voulu alors le traduire car justement c'était un texte qui éveillait en moi de fortes réactions, comme quoi on n'est jamais neutre en tant que traducteur. Or le livre, publié à Paris, semble être « filtré » par une langue libre, riche en registres, permettant de dire facilement le non-dit. En essayant de me trouver une juste place pour amener ce livre le plus fidèlement possible vers le lecteur albanais, le concept de *triangle culturel* en traduction a commencé à s'esquisser comme un trajet parcouru quotidiennement entre

1. le pays d'origine de l'auteur, l'Algérie;
2. le pays qui l'a publié, la France;
3. et le pays de la traductrice et de la diffusion de la traduction, l'Albanie.

autrement dit entre

1. la culture de l'auteur: maghrébine, algérienne, musulmane;
2. la culture du lecteur auquel était destinée cette publication: européenne, française, majoritairement chrétienne;
3. et la culture du lecteur de la traduction: balkanique située entre l'orient et l'occident, albanaise, au passé oriental, majoritairement musulmane;

mais aussi entre:

1. l'expression française, écrite par un maghrébin, mêlée de mots arabes;
2. la langue française destinée à un lecteur français, révisée peut-être par l'éditeur;

3. et la langue albanaise, relevant d'un groupe à part dans la famille des langues indo-européennes, mais avec un lexique assez riche en provenance de la langue turque en raison des cinq siècles passés sous la domination de l'Empire ottoman.

Sur cette carte géographique, culturelle et linguistique à trois caps, le transfert n'est pas simple. Ce ne sont pas des mots que l'on doit transposer mais des mondes. Les mots ouvrent des mondes et le traducteur doit ouvrir le même monde que celui que l'auteur a ouvert. Comme le dit Umberto Eco (2003), les traducteurs ne sont pas des peseurs de mots, mais des peseurs d'âme et dans cette histoire de passage d'un monde à l'autre, tout est affaire de négociation. Le traducteur est celui qui sait bien négocier avec les exigences du monde de départ pour déboucher sur un monde d'arrivée.

Dans notre cas, la négociation s'est située entre
– les références culturelles de l'auteur qui appartiennent à son pays d'origine, à sa religion, à l'histoire de son pays,
– les explicitations que l'auteur fait pour le lecteur de la publication en France,
– et références culturelles du public de la traduction qui se rapproche de la culture d'origine par son histoire et par les aspects religieux mais qui est assez familier aussi avec la culture européenne et chrétienne grâce à sa position géographique (en Europe) et à sa diversité religieuse.

Lors de cette traduction, je me suis posée à plusieurs reprises la question du monde que j'étais en train d'amener dans mon propre univers. Ainsi, dès la lecture, me trouvant sur le terrain religieux du roman, j'ai été confrontée à des notions plutôt chrétiennes comme: "*créature satanique*", "*cataclysme*", "*blasphème*", "*condamnation divine*", *manger avec la main gauche était un acte* "*illicite*", "*pêché*", "*diable*", "*enfer*":... tout ceci dans un contexte bien musulman. Mais il y avait aussi l'opposé: l'auteur utilise souvent le mot arabe "*roumi*" pour désigner les Français, leur langue, leurs moeurs; certes dans la culture musulmane albanaise, il existe également des mots pour désigner péjorativement les chrétiens (notamment *kaur*).

Ce livre d'expression française n'est pas une littérature de France tout en étant destiné à un public plutôt français. On ressent ainsi le souci de l'auteur de rendre certaines choses plus explicites *[l'Aid al- Kebir, la fête de Mouton; le fils de Flen-ben-Flen, (le fils d'un tel); ma tante Louloua, -son beau nom signifie "la perle" en arabe; elle était fière de son nom, Sama, qui signifie "le ciel" en arabe; la célèbre Alfiat ibn Malek (mille vers résumant toutes les règles, exceptions et nuances de la grammaire arabe)]*. Cela n'exclut pas cependant un public francophone (notamment maghrébin) qui lirait pour connaitre surtout la position de l'auteur et sa façon de raconter et qui, contrairement au lecteur français, ne découvre pas cette réalité mais un point de vue. Quant au public de la traduction, il appréhende une culture et une vision, doublement « traduite » d'abord en français puis en albanais.

Au moment de la réécriture du texte en albanais, une troisième culture est intervenue. Les correspondances albanaises qui me revenaient pour rendre les références religieuses étaient également chrétiennes. Or, parlant d'un monde musulman, cela sentait faux. En Albanie, même si la religion n'occupe pas une place importante dans la vie sociale, la religion musulmane, pour des raisons historiques, reste la religion majoritaire. Force est de souligner que la langue albanaise ne manque pas d'un lexique riche en expressions relevant du monde musulman, héritage de sa période turque. C'est dans ce fond que j'ai puisé pour traduire toutes les références, les éléments du discours musulman de l'original. J'ai traduit ce livre en période de ramadan, profitant de cette coïncidence pour suivre des émissions, des activités de la communauté musulmane et prenant en notes des mots, des expressions décrivant en albanais des situations, des notions, des rites musulmans, que j'essayais d'insérer ensuite dans mon texte. Par ces interprétations, je faisais une sorte de court-circuit dans ce triangle qui partait de l'Algérie, passait par la France, pour arriver en Albanie qui rejoignait à nouveau le Maghreb grâce à la proximité de son lexique religieux.

J'ai suivi la même approche, pour décrire/traduire des objets, des habitudes, des actions, comme par exemple, la *« méida »* que l'auteur, après l'avoir écrit en italique comme une parole étrangère au français, se voit obligé de l'expliquer comme une *«petite table ronde basse»* autour de laquelle se réunit la famille pour manger. Preuve s'il en est de la conscience qu'il avait du public français, proche par la langue, étranger par la culture. Pas de dilemme pour le texte albanais: j'ai supprimé la partie explicative, remplaçant le mot arabe « *méida* » par le mot correspondant *« sofra »* qui désigne en albanais exactement le même type de table utilisée jadis par nos paysans. De même pour les ustensiles de la maison qui nécessitent à chaque fois une explication, comme par exemple le mot arabe « *gassaa* » (aussi en italiques) pour lequel on a en albanais le correspondant « *sahan* », mot archaïque, dérivé du turc, qui rend bien l'ambiance rurale et orientale du livre.

La démarche s'est compliquée lorsque le texte original abordait un autre tabou: le sexe. Dans ma réécriture, je rejoignais alors le contexte de départ non plus par les mots, ni par les ressemblances situationnelles, mais par les interdits. Les scènes érotiques abondent, non pas comme une obsession sexuelle mais comme une « allégorie philosophique et sociale, voire politique», selon Max Véga-Ritter parlant d'un autre roman de Zaoui *Les gens du parfum,* je dirais comme une juste réponse à «l'hypocrisie du village, où les hommes se livrent à la fornication et les femmes aux tromperies» (A.Z). Le français permet à l'auteur de se régaler en mots et expressions sensuelles/ sexuelles sans tomber en aucun cas dans la vulgarité. Tâche difficile de les traduire en albanais où les tabous d'une société traditionnellement conservatrice ont privé la parole d'un aussi riche registre qu'en français pour exprimer des sensations et des scènes érotiques que tout le monde pourtant connaît. Contrairement à l'auteur qui avait fait le choix de la langue de l'Autre, dans mon réécriture je n'avais plus cette possibilité. Le risque était de tomber dans le vulgaire. En albanais, les mots désignant les sexes masculin ou féminin, ou l'acte sexuel même, font généralement partie d'un registre vulgaire. Il est difficile, voire impossible, de trouver des dénominations qu'on pourrait utiliser sans risquer de provoquer des réactions indésirables. En outre, personnellement j'ai grandi et vécu dans ce pays où dominaient ces tabous. Il n'était évident ni pour moi ni pour mon lecteur de « libérer ma langue », sans choquer. La seule solution était de recourir à des mots génériques (assez limités d'ailleurs) comme « sexe, pénis » pour la « verge », mais sans solutions correspondantes pour « baiser », « conin », qui dans le texte original ne marquaient point la vulgarité alors qu'en albanais, ils auraient connoté la grossièreté. Pour ne pas abuser du mot « sexe », j'ai eu recours à des épithètes qualitatifs (par exemple *« i ngrefosur »* pour désigner le sexe en érection), des synonymes infantiles puisque le héros est un adolescent (comme « *bibilushi* » équivalent de « zizi »), ou des métaphores allégoriques (« *u tendos si hell* » qui montrent l'excitation de l'organe masculin). Des lecteurs ont confirmé la pleine présence de l'érotisme dans la traduction. Ce n'est que grâce aux interprétations des scènes, des émotions et en plongeant presque dans les mêmes sensations et visualisations, que je crois avoir pu traduire l'érotisme de l'original aussi fidèlement que possible, non seulement par des mots érotiques mais surtout par des situations et les effets et émotions qu'elles suscitent, comme dans les extraits suivant: par exemple p. 88, *L'œil du loup: sous sa robe en soie fine bleu clair, son corps rose, svelte, superbement sculpté, me paraissait presque nu, savoureux et appétissant./ Syri i ujkut: ndën fustanin e saj prej mëndafshi të hollë të kaltër, kurmi rozë, i hajthëm, mrekullisht i gdhendur, m'u duk thuajse lakuriq, kullonte e të hapte oreksin.*); ou encore p. 114: *Quand Louloua arriva à ranimer mon intérieur, quand ma verge fut devenue ferme et bien tendue, elle le nicha doucement et délicatement entre ses gros seins gonflés/ Kur Luluaja arriti të ma ngjallte shpirtin, kur penisi m'u kreshpërua e m'u tendos si hell, ajo me lezet e futi ëmbëlsisht mes gjinjve të saj të mëdhenj e të fryrë.)*

Dans les études qui abordent la littérature maghrébine d'expression française, on justifie souvent l'emploi de « la langue de l'Autre » pour critiquer, pour se libérer, pour exprimer des choses qu'on ne pourrait pas exprimer dans sa propre langue (pour diverses raisons). Ces écrivains quand ils ne peuvent pas fuir la réalité de leur pays, s'exilent dans une autre langue car leur langue maternelle les rend plus vulnérables aux préjugés et jugements de leur propre société.

L'autocensure a poussé Zaoui plutôt vers l'expression française plutôt qu'arabe. Au même titre que, par exemple, l'écrivain Altiq Rahimi qui a reçu le prix Goncourt 2008 avec un livre dont les évènements se passent quelque part en Afghanistan: *« Si j'avais écrit ce livre en persan, j'aurais adopté un langage pudique et pratiqué l'autocensure.»* Moi-même, j'ai ressenti cette autocensure au niveau des tabous sexuels tandis que j'étais libre de choisir mes mots et mes expressions pour les termes de religion ou de politique.

3. Métaphorisation et intertextualité: lecture de la Goutte d'Or

Le livre de Tournier peut se décomposer en trois parties: les origines et le milieu natal d'Idriss, son départ du Sahara et son arrivée en France (p. 60-116), puis le séjour à Paris, toujours à la recherche de cette photo qui lui a comme volé son identité.

La Goutte d'Or, à la fois titre et un des fils du roman, est également tripartite: elle est la « bulla aurea » (p. 103), symbole de pureté et de liberté de l'enfance passée dans la tribu saharienne, sans images (sauf une photo de combattants de la seconde guerre mondiale, précieusement portée par l'oncle Mogadem puis épinglée au mur, p. 15 et 55); elle est le bijou, d'abord aperçu sur le ventre d'une danseuse noire – « émanation d'un monde sans image » (p. 31), talisman réconfortant (p. 96) puis donné comme paiement à une prostituée de Marseille (p. 113-114) et ensuite retrouvé dans une vitrine de la place Vendôme (p. 219); enfin, elle est la référence à une rue du quartier Barbès où habite Etienne Milan, photographe et collectionneur de mannequins de vitrine, dans un appartement situé dans « un immeuble délabré » (p. 177).

Certains éléments (soldats africains engagés dans la deuxième guerre mondiale; danseuse noire, représentante d'un groupe distinct des oasiens et des nomades, pendant positive du voleur Toubou (p. 70) et de l'employé de l'hôtel Rym qui chasse Idriss (p. 74); quartier parisien d'immigrés) ne sont explicités ni dans le texte de départ ni dans la traduction – chaque lecteur inférant selon ses propres connaissances et expériences pour comprendre allusions et connotations. Autre image-clé: celle du désert, doublement représenté, entre surface et profondeur, comme d'autres traits du roman, par exemple la nature double de Barberousse (p. 32-47) qui finalement se regarde et s'admet tel qu'il est, après épreuve. Aux représentations du vécu (p. 9-11) se superposent des représentations construites du Sahara, non identifiables, non reconnaissables par Idriss, par exemple au musée de Béni Abbès (p. 75-79: « Sahara empaillé »), dans le studio du photographe Mustapha à Béchar où le désert « en trompe l'œil » sert de toile de fonds pour tirer des portraits (p. 82-86), sur une pancarte publicitaire d'une oasis, « image de rêve » (p. 106-107). Entre le simulacrum et l'hyper-réel de Baudrillard (1981: 10, 157-163), Tournier s'interroge sur les rapports ambigus entre réalité et image, analogue au questionnement d'Idriss sur sa photo de passeport (p. 94-95 et 100: « ce n'est pas à moi de ressembler à ma photo. C'est ma photo qui doit me ressembler, non? »). L'essence du moi ne saurait être altérée par un changement extérieur, de surface, comme l'image (ou photo ou peinture) « douée d'une force mauvaise », ne saurait révéler une identité profonde – au contraire du culte occidental des images (mirages) qui donne à croire que l'illusion de la reproduction est la réalité, qu'en recréant cette réalité, on fait oeuvre artistique (p. 86). Dans cette série d'initiation à la problématique de la représentation, on peut ajouter le message publicitaire du soda aux fruits « Palmeraie » (p. 143) où Idriss n'est plus spectateur médusé, choqué (p. 142) – « le Sahara, j'ai appris ça en France » (p. 129), mais où il devrait participer à cette mystification, à cette représentation du bédouin et de son chameau qui atteint le comble de l'irréalité avec l'épisode de l'animal déambulant dans Paris, au cimetière de Montmarte, le long de la Seine, vers les abattoirs de Vaugirard, puis dans le Jardin d'Acclimatation (p. 147-149).

Le chameau, double d'Idriss dans la problématique du signe et de l'image, animal- synecdoque du désert, a une fonction référentielle: Ibrahim, ami d'enfance du personnage principal, chamelier, meurt dans un puits à cause d'une chamelle (p. 16-21); la Land Rover de la blonde décolorée qui va voler le portrait d'Idriss, n'est pas « sans affinité lointaine avec le chameau bâté » (p. 14); Idriss « s'absorbait ... dans la sculpture de chameaux ... pour jouer au nomade chaamba « (p. 23), avant donc de devenir lui-même jouet aux mains d'un producteur de publicité et animal « pomponné » auprès du « Palais des miroirs déformants » (p. 159) – la mise en scène des faussetés de l'image atteignant son paroxysme avec le moulage d'Idriss comme « mannequin du type maghrébin » (p. 176, 181-187).

Bien des métaphores sont liées au thème du désert. On en distinguera deux groupes. D'abord celles afférant à la chaleur et au soleil. Par exemple « la ligne rougeoyante des dunes » (p. 9) devenue « sanddynerna som vitglödgade höjde sig vid horisonten » (p. 7 de la traduction), c'est-à-dire des dunes chauffées à blanc, comme dans une fonderie, et se levant à l'horizon. Ou encore « quand il aperçut dans le tremblement de la terre surchauffée, glissant sur un boqueteau de tamaris, la silhouette pataude d'une Land Rover » (p. 13) rendu par « då han genom den dallrande luften som steg upp från den överhettade marken fick syn på en landrovers klumpiga silhuett, som gled fram mot backgrunden av en dunge av tamariskor» (p. 10-11). La métaphore filée du texte de départ mélange mouvement violent et chaleur émanant du sol. Le texte d'arrivée est la traduction d'une interprétation non métaphorique, décrivant le phénomène de l'air tremblant qui monte de la terre, alors que la seconde partie atténue la métaphore (la voiture ne glisse plus « sur un boqueteau de tamaris » mais « contre un fond de boqueteau de tamaris »): la vision de la Land Rover comme par magie au-dessus de la végétation est perdue. Des deux exemples ici, on ne peut tirer aucune conclusion sur les stratégies du traducteur mais l'analyse d'autres exemples confirme que la valeur stylistique et sémantique des métaphores est en général gardée, le traducteur se permettant parfois des interprétations non métaphoriques (par exemple « le soleil au sommet de sa courbe » (p. 65) est rendu par « står i zenith » (p. 64)).

Le second groupe de métaphores porte sur le paysage et le sable: « La silhouette tourmentée de rares souches mortes » (p. 10), « l'apparition d'un fantôme d'oasis » (p. 65), « derrière une rangée de palmiers lépreux » (p. 65), « cette montagne instable et tendre ... en cascades blondes » (p. 73), « à l'est moutonnait ... l'échine d'or d'une infinité d'autres dunes, une mer de sable ... la toison verte de la palmeraie » (p. 73), etc. « La crète, une arête rigoureusement dessinée, qu'un friselis provoqué par le vent ne cessait de peigner et d'aiguiser » (p. 72) est devenu (p. 72): « ... över en omsorgsfullt tecknad kam som oavbrutet slipades av den sakta brisen ». Dans la métaphore filée de départ, le friselis, personnalisé, agit comme peigne et aiguisoir, comme si la crète de dunes était faite de matière à la fois dure comme de l'acier et souple comme des cheveux. La traduction raccourcit (une crète rigoureusement dessinée incessamment aiguisée par la brise lente): arête n'a pas de correspondant direct en suédois, et friselis signifie un effet produit par la brise et non pas la brise elle-même. Pour décrire cet effet, une description aurait été nécessaire. « Kam » en suédois est polysémique, comme crête: il signifie l'excroissance sur la tête du coq, l'arête d'une vague, la ligne de faîte d'une montagne, mais aussi, et en premier, il veut dire peigne. Pouvait-on peigner le peigne?

Des nuances fines peuvent ainsi se perdre; des éléments laissent place à des interprétations divergentes. Ajoutées aux allusions citées plus haut sur le désert en général, ces transformations dans la traduction donnent à lire un texte différent, à des degrés divers selon les connaissances encyclopédiques, linguistiques et culturelles du lecteur, ses capacités à lire entre les lignes.

Si on considère maintenant la photo/l'image et l'oeil/le portrait, on constate la forte récurrence non pas du rejet mais de la distanciation à l'image, surface au « pouvoir maléfique » (p. 15), « malfaisant » (p. 207) qui ne saurait représenter la profondeur – opposition qui hante le récit de Barberousse (p. 32-47). La dépendance image-réalité (ressemblance/identité), propre à notre culture, ne peut créer que l'aliénation d'Idriss, marqué par l'Islam et son interdit du portrait, ou son trouble quand il est pris pour Ismaël (p. 93): il ne peut se représenter ses propres traits. Il ne peut donc se voir. Dans le récit du portrait interdit de « la reine blonde » (p. 203-216), l'artiste peintre ne peut finir son travail, préférant se pendre (p. 205). Des représentations par la photo, le moulage, le portrait, les mots, on ne peut se libérer qu'en lettré, avec la magie de la calligraphie (p. 210 et suivantes)

Les métaphores de l'image, incluant les thèmes de la photo, du miroir, de la lumière, du regard, de l'œil – souvent « le mauvais » (p. 15, 40, 215), des signes, de la calligraphie, sont nombreuses. On n'en citera que quelques cas, à titre d'exemples et sans prétention à la généralisation de leur stratégie de traduction (entre autres: glissement sémantique, explicitation, métaphorisation lexicalisée, traduction littérale): « son image roulait enfermée dans le boitier de l'appareil » (p. 15), « toute image avantageuse est grosse de menace » (p. 24), « l'image que j'en ferai sera lavée des salissures du moment » (p. 39), « l'image sournoise, menteuse et impérieuse » (p. 100), « certains soirs avant de me coucher, je m'en paie une énorme tranche » (p. 150), « l'effigie est verrou, l'idole prison, la figure serrure » (p. 201), etc.

Autre récurrence: la sexualité. Les trois formes, masculine, féminine et homosexuelle, sont thématisées par le mot argotique *zob* (pour pénis) d'origine arabe. C'est à la fois le marteau-piqueur qui « détruit et pénètre » (p. 218-219), « symbole du travailleur maghrébin » (p. 217), le nom propre du rabatteur-proxénète (p. 137) contre lequel Idriss va se heurter dans la séquence de la BD (p. 169-170), et une partie du nom de la danseuse noire (Zett Zobeida), porteuse de la Goutte d'Or. En suédois, la violence, le mépris qui transparaissent dans la description du travail des immigrés arabes, place Vendôme (p. 217-219), sont quasi neutralisés (« lem » pour « zob », « bryter du upp » pour « tu crèves », « räcker lang näsa » pour « tu niques », « stöldämpare » pour « fleuret », « mejseln » pour « pénétration »).

Quant à l'intertextualité fondée sur les citations et allusions parodiques à la littérature (les deux récit légendaires, Flaubert (p. 131), Voltaire (p. 140), Saint Exupéry (p. 141-142), Valéry (p. 147), Géraldy (p. 152)), à des proverbes (p. 211-214), à la litanie reprise comme leitmotiv associé à la Goutte d'Or (p. 30, 49, 96, 113, 154, 197, 220), à des chansons de Béranger, de Renaud (p. 165-169) ou d'Oum Kalsoum (p192-196), elle disparait aussi en grande partie dans la traduction puisque les notes explicatives de l'auteur sont omises, privant ainsi le lecteur suédois du jeu intertextuel.

Dernier élément à considérer quand on songe à la « traduction » des réalités d'Idriss en français puis à leur traduction en suédois: la présence de mots arabes dans le texte, en distinguant ceux empruntés et lexicalisés en français (25 au total) et ceux toujours ressentis comme étrangers (aussi au nombre de 25). Dans le premier groupe, on aurait par exemple *bled* (p. 110, 146, 190) et *zob* (ni expliqués ni mis en italique dans le texte source), *baraka* (p. 90, 127) et *méhariste*

(p. 135-136). *Bled* est rendu tel quel mais en italique (p. 108) dans un microcontexte qui précise qu'on a affaire à un lieu en Afrique du Nord et qui laisse entendre qu'on en vient sans un certain savoir-faire occidental; il est également traduit par « din by » (ton village, p. 145) et par « algeriska landsbygden » (village rural algérien, p. 189 – traduction assez restrictive puisque dans le foyer auquel il est fait allusion il n'y pas que des immigrés algériens). La *baraka* est repris formellement, y compris avec l'article (la baraka, deux fois, en italique, p. 89 – sans définition ni explicitation contextualisée). Pour *méhariste*, le mot est transcrit directement, adapté aux règles de la grammaire suédoise (« meharisterna », p. 134-135, le contexte permettant jusqu'à un certain point d'en inférer le sens: personne qui monte un chameau, mais la cooccurrence « jävla » peut laisser entendre aussi qu'il s'agirait d'un mot injurieux).

Pour les mots arabes, non signalés de manière disitinctive, comme par exemple *kanoun* et *kharbaga* (p. 190-191), *lam-alif* (p. 209), on a une transcription directe, sans explication. Le contexte immédiat suffit pour faire comprendre les fonctions remplies par ces mots (respectivement plaque chauffante, jeu, lettre de l'alphabet), mais sans autre précision sur la nature, la forme de ces items. L'effet voulu – l'exotisme – est néanmoins rendu.

Les quelques éléments et exemples cités ne suffisent pas à conclure quoi que ce soit, de façon péremptoire, sur les techniques du traducteur, encore moins sur la réception de l'œuvre. La *Goutte d'Or* prend place cependant dans les thématiques de Tournier qui a toujours mêlé mythes, images et intrigue, comme dans *Vendredi ou les limbes du Pacifique* (1967), *Le roi des Aulnes* (1970), *Les météores* (1975), *Gaspar, Melchior et Balthazar* (1980), qui a souvent combiné notes, photos et dessins (*Des clés et des serrures* (1983), *Le Vagabond immobile* (1984), *Journal de voyage au Canada* (1984)), et qui a pratiqué la photo en présentant une cinquantaine d'émissions télévisées sur des photographes, en organisant une exposition sur ses photographes préférés, en publiant un livre sur la photo *Le crépuscule des masques* (1992).

4. En guise de conclusion

Les littératures postcoloniales sont souvent présentées dans une perspective d'opposition frontale, comme si une langue-culture indienne, jamaïcaine, africaine se heurtait à une langue-culture occidentale, comme si le rapport entre les deux était un rapport hiérarchique linéaire, l'une étant subordonnée exclusivement à l'autre. Cette supposée opposition tranchée entre colonisateur et colonisé, centre et périphérie, métropole et colonie, cette hégémonie coloniale prétendument directe ne peuvent rendre compte de bien des situations mixtes, de conflits transnationaux, du dynamisme d'inter-fertilisation linguistique, culturelle, littéraire qu'on trouve aujourd'hui.

Traduction et critique postcoloniale ont traditionnellement été articulées en termes de relation de pouvoir (Niranjana 1992, Robinson 1997, Bassnett & Trivedi 1999, Tymoczko 1999, Sherry & St Pierre 2000). Dans ce cadre, la traduction aurait joué un rôle actif, univoque dans la colonisation, dans l'expansion d'une langue, contrôlant la subjectivité et les représentations du colonisé. Un certain discours postcolonial sur la traduction (littéraire) a cherché à interroger et à renverser cette asymétrie, recourant à des notions et outils analytiques comme l'interventionnisme, l'hybridité perçue comme lieu de résistance et de négociation, d'entre deux (Bhabha 1994). Les situations contemporaines de conflit, les émergences sur le devant de la scène internationale d'anciennes colonies (britanniques, françaises, portugaises, espagnoles, etc.), la reconnaissance de littératures dites naguère périphériques, ne peuvent s'expliquer aisément et exclusivement en termes d'empire, de colonisation à sens unique.

A la fin des années 1920, une stratégie particulière a été suggérée au Brésil, héritière de certains mouvements modernistes européens, pour dire une relation possible à l'autre, pour s'émanciper de sa domination: le cannibalisme ou comment assimiler, absorber la langue de cet autre pour mieux s'affirmer. Cette métaphore de l'anthropophagie a connu un certain succès « théorique » pour souligner combien le traducteur pouvait dévorer le texte original et le recréer sans se soucier des notions occidentales de fidélité, d'original, etc. (Gentzler 2008).

Dans les deux romans approchés, on a constaté comment les auteurs ont eu recours au français pour « traduire » une réalité longtemps considérée comme dominée, aliénée, et comment dès lors s'esquisse un triangle culturel plutôt qu'un duel, entre

- les réalités maghrébines, musulmanes, algériennes, à la fois arrière-plan et objet des deux récits, et touchant les conditions et contraintes religieuses, politiques, sexuelles ainsi que les représentations de soi ;
- les réalités de la réception par des lecteurs de langue française, de culture, de croyances, de valeurs différentes, et pour lesquelles les auteurs ont explicité certains éléments, en ont tu d'autres – éclairant ici une allusion, laissant là un non-dit;
- les réalités de la lecture des traductions plus ou moins distantes des réalités précédentes – l'ouvrage en albanais re-tournant, retrouvant un passé musulman plus ou moins enfoui, par delà la « traduction » française, l'ouvrage en suédois se décentrant par rapport à un héritage colonial non partagé avec les lecteurs français. Il serait intéressant de voir aussi comment par exemple la traduction anglaise du *Festin de mensonges* (*Banquet of lies*) a rendu les réa-

lités initiales du livre et comment les lecteurs de langue anglaise (britanniques et américains) ont appréhendé *La goutte d'Or* (*The Golden Droplet*). Y a-t-il eu autocensure, jusqu'à un certain point, refoulement assumé de certains traits du livre de Zaoui? Reproduction littérale des clichés et métaphores du livre de Tournier? Explicitation systématique dès qu'il n'y avait pas le sentiment d'un savoir commun, partagé?

La notion de triangle culturel n'explique pas mais permet de souligner l'expérience de la « translation » entre des mondes qui peuvent être proches ou éloignés géographiquement, historiquement, tantôt grâce à une langue intermédiaire (le français dans les deux cas étudiés), tantôt par delà cette langue. Le rapport entre l'univers de départ et celui d'arrivée n'est ni forcément direct ni nécessairement assujetti. Une langue naguère importée, imposée peut en effet dire aujourd'hui les affres de ses anciens colonisés, servant dès lors de moyen de résistance, d'émancipation.

Bibliographie

Sources primaires

Tournier, Michel. 1986. *La Goutte d'Or*. Paris: Gallimard. Edition utilisée: Folio 1908, dépôt légal: juin 2000
Tournier, Michel. 1987. *Gulddroppen*. Traduit en suédois par C.G. Bjurström. Stockholm: Bonniers.
Tournier, Michel. 1987. *The Golden Droplet*. Traduit en anglais par Barbara Wright. New York: Doubleday Publishing.
Zaoui, Amin. 2007. *Le festin de mensonges*. Paris: Fayard.
Zaoui, Amin, 2008. *Gostia e genjeshtrave*. Traduit en albanais par Mirela Kumbaro. Tirana: Editions Dituria.
Zaoui, Amin, 2008. *Banquet of Lies* (édition bilingue). Traduit en anglais par Frank Wyne. Londres: Marion boyards Publishers

Sources secondaires

Baudrillard, Jean. 1981. *Simulacres et simulations*. Paris: éditions Galilée.
Bassnett, Susan & Harish Triverdi (eds), 1999. *Post-colonial Translation: Theory and Practice*. Londres: Routledge.

Bhabha, Homi. 1994. *Location of Culture*. Londres: Routledge. Traduit en français en 2007 par Françoise Bouillot: *Lieux de la culture: une théorie postcoloniale*. Paris: Payot

Eco, Umberto, 2003, Dire quasi la stessa cosa, esperienze di traduzione, Milano, Bompiani.

Gentzler, Edwin. 2008. *Translation and Identity in the Americas*. Londres: Routledge.

Niranjana, Tewaswini.1992. Siting Translation: History, Post-structuralism and the Colonial Context. Berkeley: University of California Press.

Robinson, Douglas. 1997. *Translation and Empire*. Manchester: St Jerome.

Sherry Simon & Paul Bandia (eds), 2000. *Changing the terms. Translating in the postcolonial era*. Ottawa: Univesity Press of Ottawa.

Wohlfart, Irmengard. 2009. "Investigating a double translation of culture. The English-Maori classic postcolonail text *Potiki* and its German translation", *Target* 21 (2), 265-288.

Translation and the Dialectic of Continental Crossroads: A Case Study of Assam

Manjeet Baruah

In the recent period, if there has been a major contribution from south Asia in the field of translation study, it has been to emphasize the point that the assumption of SL-TL framework does not explain the historical role of translation in the subcontinent. It is because translation in the subcontinent has been about indigenized transcreations. Transcreations were central not only to the process of exchange between languages but also to the process of language formation itself. Between the $8^{th}/9^{th}$ centuries AD and $16^{th}/17^{th}$ centuries AD, most the 'Indian' languages that one comes across today were formed during this period. Transcreations were not the dynamic exchange between two languages existing a priori; it was about being a part of the very process of language formation. However, in the paper, we would take a step further and argue that such processes need to be situated in frameworks which are not confined to the understanding of language per se. How do we conceptualise the process of communication when it takes place not through language per se but through shared forms of knowledge, especially when these shared forms of knowledge does not exist within linguistic structures of languages but are spread across the languages? The question could become even more pertinent when different communities, conscious of their 'language', participate in the development of these knowledge forms not only to communicate but also as the means to retain their diversity/difference. The issue can be posed vis-à-vis the case of transcreation and formation of 'Indian' languages too, though it isn't being posed in such a manner. Could such a position on how to approach translation help one see beyond the exchange relations between two languages (and cultures studied based on languages/literatures) and incorporate domains which have differently operated, though in terms of transfer and communication, i.e. translation? It may be noted that, of late, in works such as those of Gentzler[1], the recognition of such processes has led to revisiting of the fundamental question in translation studies, namely what is translation?

---

1   Gentzler, Edwin (2008) Translation and Identity in the Americas: New Directions in Translation Theory, London: Routledge.

Situating the region

The paper is an exploration of the relation between translation and social diversity in the trans-Brahmaputra valley, comprising mainly the valley of the river Brahmaputra and its adjoining hills, located at the crossroad of South Asia, South East Asia and East Asia. The area is also what largely constitutes the region of Assam in the modern times. Spatially, the area is an arrangement of valley, foothills and hills. The narrow Brahmaputra valley created by the large braided river system of the Brahmaputra originating in Tibet, has to its north the lower Himalayas which connects it to Bhutan, Tibet and China while the Patkai ranges connects it to Burma or Myanmar and present day Bangladesh to the south/south east. Socio-spatial relations in the area had been historically dominated by the two mountain systems of the lower Himalayas and the Patkai with the braided river system of the Brahmaputra between the two. The three geographical formations together are also referred to as the trans-Brahmaputra valley. Historically, the trans-Brahmaputra valley had been both a route of migration as well as destination of migration for different communities. As a result, the area experienced the socio-cultural impact of South Asia (the Gangetic area of the Indian subcontinent), South East Asia (the Shan highlands of northern Burma) and East Asia (Tibet and China). Three cases of the impact are outlined below.

(1) The Bodo-Kacharis were one of the earliest settlers in the NER. The migration was however mostly in the pre-historical times. The Bodo-Kacharis today are spread across the entire geographical formation which constitutes NER as well as in its adjoining countries. The Bodo-Kacharis trace their origin in Tibet (from the Bods), from where they had spread or migrated to different parts of the NER. They are also found in north Bengal, given its proximity to the lower Himalayas, and also in present day Bangladesh (for example, areas such as Mymensing). Many of the communities inhabiting NER, especially in the valleys today, such as the Bodos, the Sonowals, the Chutiyas, the Mataks, the Garos, the Dimasas and others trace their ethnicity to the Bodo-Kachari origin. The Bodo-Kacharis have been one of the most significant groups of people that have shaped the history of the region. For example, a large number of languages spoken in the NER belong to the Tibeto-Burman language group. The spread of the language group had much to do with the migration and spreading out of the Bodo-Kacharis. What we need to remember here is that the very name 'Tibeto-Burman' devised in the 19th century to classify the language properties of the region indicates how implicit in it is the geographical area that the language group incorporates or refers to stretches from Tibet to Burma or Myanmar. When we try to see the impact of this condition in everyday life, the most visible im-

pact can be seen, for example, in the names of rivers, places, hills, etc throughout the NER. Most rivers flowing down the lower Himalayas or down the Patkai, begin with 'di' such as Dihing, Dibang, Disang, etc, 'di' meaning water in Tibeto-Burman languages.

While the Bodo-Kachari migration into Assam was from the north, the series of migrations from upper Burma or Myanmar into the valleys (especially of present day Assam) during the historical period were equally crucial. The most famous of these migrations have been the migration of the Ahoms in the 13th century. The migration of the Ahoms was a part of the Indo-Burma migration tradition, and also a part of the Indo-Burma worldview. This worldview got recorded in their *buranji* chronicles, one of the earliest prose forms of writing in the region and which grew into a very large body of literature by the 18th century. The Ahoms had used one of the frequently used migration routes from upper Burma (Shan area) via the Patkai ranges to arrive at the eastern fringes of the Brahmaputra valley, on the southern bank of the river. The Ahoms later spread to different parts of the valley, inter-marrying with those from the Bodo-Kachari groups. Thus some of the communities like Mataks, etc are considered parts of both Bodo-Kachari and Ahom social formations at the same time.

(2) The route that the Ahoms used was extensively used by many later migrating groups such as the Singphos (who were credited with the knowledge of growing tea, from whom the Bruce brothers appropriated the knowledge after brutal war crime atrocities and commenced colonial commercial initiatives towards our now famous Assam tea variety) or the Khamptis who settled at the eastern fringes of the valley in later centuries. The route was also used in the Burmese invasions of the Ahom kingdom in the early 19th century. The Ahom *buranjis* provide a detailed account of the Indo-Burma worldview of the Ahoms and how the Brahmaputra valley was seen as part of the larger geography to which the Ahoms from Shan area of upper Burma also belonged to. For example, in one of the most authoritative and early *buranjis*, the *Deodhai Oxom Buranji*, the entire geographical stretch from upper Burma to Patkai to the eastern Brahmaputra valley area are not only seen as part of their mythical geography but also where the political ambitions of the different Shan clans can be legitimately played out. Thus, while in the modern period, the migration of Ahoms into Assam came to be seen as migration from outside, in the *buranjis* of the Ahoms, it was movement or migration but *within* their own notional geographical space and not beyond it. Ironically, what modern nationhood has systematically done is to legitimize the *buranjis*, a massive literary tradition, as relics of the past, its worldview to be treated only as history! But at the same time, the Ramayana tradition that entered from the Indo-Gangetic belt in Assam continues to be taught as part of our living tradition! What is this rationality of modern nationhood that teaches us to abhor today a

worldview which was a fundamental part of our collective life and worldview? Perhaps there isn't any, and therefore the need to station the army unfailingly, every time, everywhere.

The integrated whole about the region was also there in trade and cultural practices, in other words, our material culture, for example in the culture of beads. One of the most extensive trades in which the entire NER and its adjoining areas participated was that of beads. It extended from Burma or Myanmar through the NER to Bhutan, Tibet and China and then further into Central Asia. The entire NER, its hills/mountains, foothills and valleys, participated in this widespread trade in two ways, namely through consumption and through transport. The region not only was a consumer of beads but also served as the route through which the trade took place and in which the people participated. From Bhutan, Tibet and adjoining areas of China through NER to Myanmar, the culture of bead is one of the most predominant socio-cultural forms among different communities, irrespective of the locale. Comparatively, the culture of precious metals such as gold and silver has been historically less frequent than that of beads. Stuart Blackburn in one of his studies on 'Memories of Migration'[2] has pointed out that trade and bead culture was closely tied with notions of shared geography among the people as well as memories of shared ancestry.

(3) However, this condition of notions of shared geography and shared ancestry did not lead to different communities becoming same. Each community maintained its distinct identity but at the same time lived with shared notions of space and ancestry, retained and passed down in time through their folklore and origin myths. Blackburn highlights three points pertaining to trade in bead and the development of bead culture in the region. Firstly, he shows that the extensive trade in bead was linked to the geographical location of the region in the zone of bead trade. Secondly, the trade was linked or became linked to notions of shared geography and ancestry among the different communities. That is why the trade was linked to patterns of migrations and settlement in the region. Thirdly, the bead culture became a common culture throughout the entire region. But each community developed its own distinct bead pattern, which Blackburn argues, shows how notions of commonality and distinctiveness were part of the history of this larger geographical formation. A similar condition can also be seen in the textile culture of the entire region. It is undeniable that its geometric textile patterns, whether in cotton or woollen, distinguishes the region from all its three neighbouring continental blocks. But despite the commonality of geometric patterns, each community weaves its own arrangement of patterns. The specifics of each

---

2   Blackburn, Stuart, (2003/2004) 'Memories of Migration', *EBHR*, 25/26, pp. 15-60.

community are impossible to comprehend unless the overall geometric textile patterns practiced in the entire region is taken into account.

What the three cases, or processes, make amply evident is that as continental crossroad, the trans-Brahmaputra valley was marked by diversity in social composition. Yet at the same time, it had also emerged as a historical region. The emergence as a region was based on the very nature of its historical geography. While in colonial literature, the region was referred to as 'frontier', which it was made into for the first time during the period, in many contemporary literatures, it is referred to as 'borderland'[3]. The problem in both the approaches is that they assume an idea of mainland or centre, to which the region was either 'frontier' or 'borderland'. But if we move into the pre-colonial period, and try to interpret it from within that period, the region was neither 'frontier' nor 'borderland' to any adjacent centre.

Therefore, in a discussion on translation and accommodation of diversity, the challenge for us is how to situate translation in such a context of region formation and practice of socio-spatial relations. We take as case the shared domain of Assamese language and narrative forms in the pre-colonial period. The first text of grammar of Assamese language came out in 1849 through the labours of the Baptist missionary Nathan Brown. It became the beginning of devising a procedure of language use in Assamese. Prior to the 19th century, it is difficult to identify a uniform language use in the trans-Brahmaputra valley. The difference in language use was at different levels. The tradition of language use found in the western part of the valley, as in the neo-vaishnava literatures was largely shaped by the Indo-Gangetic worldview. In contrast, the language use found in the Buranji tradition of the eastern part of the valley had clear signs of influence of South East Asian worldview. The difference between the two language uses was also at the morphological and phonological levels. It is therefore plausible to argue that the two traditions of language use were indeed distinct and were shaped by the two different worldviews. In contemporary terms, they would be language 'variants'. But it is equally important to note that there were also examples of the two traditions existing within the same text. For example, S.K. Bhuyan, the noted scholar of first half of the 20th century spent a lifetime collecting oral ballads from different parts of the valley, especially from interior areas of the valley. In 1924, he brought out a ballad called Barphukanar Geet (or the Songs of Barphukan). The ballad was on the events leading to the Burmese attacks on the valley in the early 19th century. Bhuyan collected and collated the ballad with other such oral ballads on the theme and showed how the ballad as an oral narrative on

---

3 Baruah, Sanjib (Ed.) (2009) *Beyond Counter Insurgency: Breaking the Impasse in North East.* New Delhi: Oxford University Press.

the theme could be taken as a representative sample. There were two notable features in the ballad. Firstly, unlike the colonial records which recorded the Burmese attack as devastating for the valley (which was popularised later in 'modern' Assamese literature), the ballad (and other such ballads) treated the attack as an event within the shared socio-spatial relations on either side of the Patkai mountains. The attacks, therefore, was part of long history of shared relations across shared notions of space and society. The second feature was that though the narrative was shaped by the South East Asian worldview, the language use was that of the western form of Assamese.

Importantly, there are no evidences to suggest that the language itself was referred to in the period as 'Assamese'. In fact, the language carried no name and operated as a practice of communication. The language and narratives that were practiced in the western part of the valley (as seen in the devotional neo-vaishnavite literatures) showed clear signs of extensive borrowings from the numerous social groups of the Bodo-Kachari family, despite the Indo-Gangetic worldview with which it was infused. Similarly, the language and narratives practiced in the eastern valley were replete with syntactic, morphological and phonological impact of the social groups inhabiting the area. The namelessness of the language was also what allowed diverse social groups to participate in its practice. The literatures from within the trans-Brahmaputra valley referred to the region as Axom or Aham, and the language was referred to as that spoken in Axom or Aham. The participatory scope of the language was what allowed different communities of the trans-Brahmaputra valley to use the language in different forms, whether within the valley or on the northern and southern ranges. Brown's book of grammar was a beginning when a practice of communication was being transformed into a linguistic structure. It marked the beginning of 'language' vis-à-vis 'dialects', 'pidgins' and 'creoles'. It was also a beginning when practice of communication was being framed within the confines of *a* domain, i.e. 'Assamese' language.

Throughout the last quarter of the 19th century and the first half of the 20th century, it was from this premise (of framing a shared practice within the specific domain of language) that 'modern historical' studies of language and literature were initiated. Multiple practices of assamese was amply overlooked and the focus came to be placed on tracing how the modern linguistic structure came into existence. It was assumed that the modern linguistic structure alone can help identify the Assamese language and that a teleological history of that structure can be identified. Ironically, it was also during this period that some of the fiercest debates on the linguistic structure as Assamese and on the possibility of identifying a 'history' of that linguistic structure took place in the pages of influential periodicals like the *Bahni*. After Independence, the Indian state sought to organise its different regions on the criterion of language. Conceptually, it was a major shift from the colonial policy of creating provinces out of the subcontinent. But the criterion of language was in reality the criterion of linguistic structures across the subcontinent, many of which were devised only in the 18th/19th century.

In the case of the trans-Brahmaputra valley, the impact of the state endorsement of linguistic structures as languages was two-fold. Assamese as a shared practice of communication, marked with a dynamic praxis of transfer and communication in inter-community relations, came be officially replaced by the idea of language domain, i.e. what did not fit into the linguistic structure became different languages, either having their own linguistic structures, or would need to develop it if the 'transition' was being made from oral to written culture. In linguistics, they came be seen as cases of language shift or language maintenance. Those which struggled to make the 'transition', such as Deori, Mising, etc., suffered becoming 'endangered' or 'vulnerable' languages. But the process also got entwined with the politics of ethnic identify, and therefore, on the basis of language as different from one another, they became markers of conflicting politics of identity. The conflict was over (non-existing) ethnic space for each ethnicity. The difference provided each its peculiarity, which became its atom of homogeneity, and thereby its self definition. It provided each its 'order' vis-à-vis the 'flux' in lack of being able to define one's identity. To be remembered here is that the idea or consciousness of difference was never subverted in pre-colonial practice of Assamese as shared practice of communication. What assamese facilitated was a dialectic of communication across the diversity, which had also allowed the diversity to exist and reproduce itself. When assamese became Assamese, the biggest casualty was this dialectic of communication, which had been historically central to the socio-spatial relations that comprised the continental crossroad of the valley. It was also this dialectic which had allowed the diverse to exist in the same and limited geographical space of the valley without conflict on the question of difference.

If we are correct in the line of argument that we are following, it is possible to argue the implausibility of studying historical continental crossroads like the trans-Brahmaputra valley as well as the ruptures caused in its modern transformations through domains of language, as is understood in modern times. One of the reasons why, at the level of discourse, there has been a breakdown of communication among the communities of the area has been due to the framework of approaching the issue of communication. For example, if communication of the crossroad is seen in terms of narratives rather than languages, it becomes evident that these narratives were forms which were rooted in the diverse, but from which the shared forms were developed. These shared forms were practices as well as significations which could be accessed by the diverse depending upon their context. Therefore, whether the western or the eastern practice of assamese or the dynamic inter-situatedness of the two as in the oral ballads were accessed by different clusters of communities based their respective contexts and worldviews, while they were also bearer of significations which could be comprehended by the diverse. These were possible because, as stated, the diverse participated in the development of the praxis. It may be necessary not to see this process of communication as part of the larger structure of the crossroad (parts and whole relation of structuralism). As a crossroad receiving frequent migrations and being a route of migration, it is necessary to approach the crossroad and the communication process therein as an open ended praxis, in which the diverse, remaining diverse, came together due to necessities of the historical geography, to develop shared forms of practices. If not language, and if not the notion of crossroad as structure, couldn't the framework of translation, with its embedded premise of transfer and communication, be the most suitable approach to understand process of communication and development of shared forms of practices in the area? But wouldn't then the current South Asian emphasis in translation or transcreation as part of process of language formation and not only as exchanges between two a priori existing languages, needs revision, to take translation beyond the confines of language and into the larger issues of region formation?

An on-going case study

It is possible to identify the processes noted above in practices in the contemporary times in the area? In one of such on-going studies of indigenous knowledge and translation in the trans-Brahmaputra valley, an attempt is being made to study the processes as it operates in the contemporary times, especially after the politics of linguistic onslaught has already occurred, more so in the past fifty years. It was posed whether indigenous knowledge exists as a repository or shared pool to which different communities speaking different languages and practicing different modes of everyday and social existence have participated in developing and access the knowledge as part of inter-community relation. The idea of translation experimented in the survey was that translation in this case was not about translating from one 'text' into another. On the contrary, it was about different communities speaking different languages generating a shared or common resource (of knowledge) which provides the platform for communication and exchange relations. In other words, it was taken as case of diverse sources leading to development of an unique and shared element (target) across the diversity. It was posed that if that indeed was the case, then translation was involved in not transferring a matter from text A to text B but was involved in transferring matter from diverse sources into something common for the entire diversity involved in its development. To test the hypothesis, a preliminary survey was conducted in which the people were interviewed with three criteria of information sought. They were in terms of nomenclature, means and methods of preparation and markets and communication. Under nomenclature, a wide range of names and terms such as tools of material life, expressions, names of geographical forms such as valleys or mountains, etc were used. Under means and methods of preparation, cuisines, medicines (not factory made medicines), handloom and handicrafts etc were asked. Under markets and communications, information was collected on languages used based on nature of trade and social background of trader. By the 21st century, the idea of Assamese as distinct and different from other 'languages' of the region already came to be established as a political discourse. Therefore, three communities who use more than one 'language' (along with Assamese) in their everyday and public life were identified, namely the Bodo, the Mising and the tea plantation labour community. The information on strategies adopted by the communities vis-à-vis nomenclature, means and methods of preparation and markets and communication was stratified along profile of the respondent, context of use and memory of since when used in the way they conceive it to have been used. In the survey, indigenous knowledge (in the valley) was not treated as abstract forms, but as nomenclatures practiced to communicate in everyday or social life, as knowledge of cuisines, medicines, handicraft etc practiced in everyday or social life and as language strategies used to practice exchange relations in local markets.

The survey is still on-going, but some of the early results do substantiate the hypothesis behind the survey. It also substantiates the argument made in the early part of the essay, namely that Assamese in the trans-Brahmaputra valley historically has largely been a shared practice which is differently employed by different communities and in different contexts rather than being a linguistically structured 'language' per se. This may also be taken as statement on the fact that modern Assamese language as is practiced in written writings could be far removed from the practice of assamese by different communities in reality, who together after all comprise the Assamese people.

For each of the three communities, the early results show that their indigenous knowledge in nomenclature, means and methods of preparation and market and communication is not composed of *a particular* knowledge per se. In many cases, each of the community (respondents) was conscious of the 'ethnic' particularity of their knowledge. In other words, they were aware that they had their own 'ethnic' word base to communicate and express their own means and methods of preparation different from others, or their own languages to negotiate exchange relations. However, whether practiced in everyday or social life, it was found that they universally deployed knowledge forms which were common to all communities inhabiting the trans-Brahmaputra valley. What was unique to these shared knowledge forms was that their signification was understood by the diverse communities though each community could have its own particularity while practicing it. The shared signification of these knowledge forms could be in terms of context of use, for example, in markets and communication, or in terms of 'memory' of 'evolution' in ways of celebrating seasons. In the early results of the survey, however, there were also cases when the 'ethnic' particularities were largely lost (to the respondents) and only the shared knowledge forms, or the shared significations of the knowledge forms, had come to constitute the practice of everyday or social life for the people. For example, these may be in terms of names of food items, or notions of distance or quantifications or ways of celebrating seasons, etc.

In one of the perceptive studies on the idea of Assamese in the recent times, Chandan Sharma's *Who is an Assamese?*[4] raises the basic question of how does one conceptualise Assamese. Sharma points out that though using the modern language standard of Assamese is treated as a major criterion to identify who is an Assamese, the criterion is more of one aiming to *create* Assamese, influenced by one of the discourses of identity, rather than being one which can actually help identify who is an Assamese. The problem with the discourse seeking to create Assamese is that it is based on negating the historical process of Assamese emerging and surviving as a nameless shared practiced as discussed in our earlier section, the term 'Assamese' being of modern coinage. In this regard, even in the early findings of the survey, there are numerous cases when the respondents identified themselves as Bodo, or Mising, etc. But they identified or conceived of the knowledge forms that they practice as Assamese. There were respondents who stated that they had forgotten their own 'ethnic' knowledge forms (of the given classifications in the interview schedule) and only remembered the Assamese knowledge forms. But as indicated earlier, the Assamese knowledge forms which were being referred to were nothing but the shared knowledge forms, or the shared significations of the knowledge forms, in which diverse communities have had participated in developing and keeping in use.

We now make two contentions, and through them, try to expose the problem of situating these shared knowledge forms in inter-community relations. Firstly, we contend that the shared knowledge forms, whether of nomenclature to communicate or express, of means and methods of preparation or of communication strategies in local markets, are not practiced through the framework of 'a' language.

---

4   Sharma, Chandan Kr. (2008) *Axomiya Kun?* (Who is an Assamese?), Guwahati: Span Publication.

In that case, it could be more plausible to argue that language may be used as one of the tools to understand the practice, language too being one of the components in the practice. The caution to be remembered could be that language does not comprise the practice. Secondly, the other caution to be equally remembered is that information of the research on the three communities is not about how communication and exchange occur at language borders, i.e. peripheral spaces (vis-à-vis core language spaces) wherein more than one language group occupies the space with none being the dominant. As a result, as seen in such cases core and/vs. periphery language use areas, language use is largely multi-lingual, gradually shifting into one of the languages depending upon the utility power of the respective languages[5]. But having taken into account the two contentions, the problem remains that what could be that conceptual space in which the shared knowledge forms are placed?

Two kinds of 'facts' from the early results of the survey may help us address the question. The information collected indicate that the respondents do identify what are the shared knowledge forms, but importantly, they also situate them in terms of language, namely Assamese language. The other 'fact' is that precisely because the Assamese language largely comprises the shared knowledge forms, they perceive that it has increased the vulnerability of their own 'ethnic' languages. Both Bodo and Mising are considered 'endangered/vulnerable' languages of the valley. In general, one of the frequent frameworks to analyse such 'facts' has been that of language shift and language conservation. Due to the predominance of the Assamese language, it has come to replace or substitute most other 'ethnic' languages from the use sphere, which in turn has pushed many of these 'ethnic' languages into the throes of endangered or vulnerable conditions even among the respective native speakers of the languages. However, our argument would be that this conceptual framework itself is a part of the problem rather than being the analysis of the problem. For example, in most existing older documentations, Bihu had been the shared signifier of celebrating the season of spring in the valley. In the survey, when the respondents refer to Bihu, they refer to its shared signification of nature of celebrating spring, but they also refer to it aware that Bihu is now an Assamese word signifying only certain forms of celebrating spring. Thus, they express their inability to define how they celebrate spring. This inability, in turn, gets perceived as an indicator of the vulnerability of their language vis-à-vis the Assamese language.

Is it possible, therefore, firstly to revisit the question of continental crossroads and processes of socio-spatial relations and culture therein from a perspective

---

5   Williams, Colin H. (Ed) (1988) *Language in Geographic Context*, Cleveland and Philadelphia: Multilingual Matters.

which is premised on ideas of transfer and communication and secondly to approach translation itself as a phenomenon with far wider scope of application than as it has been (though innovatively) applied in the subcontinent in terms of transcreation? We would argue that indeed it is possible. Continental crossroads are premised on dialectic between the diverse and the shared across the diversity. The dialectic cannot be explained *from within* the particularities of ethnic spaces or cultures alone. The attempts to do so through most of the 20th century has not resulted necessarily in cultural 'shift' as much as it has in the very breakdown of both inter-cultural communication (the high ethnic volatility has claimed thousands of lives) is as well as communication within a culture, as in the case of explaining celebrating spring. We would therefore argue that the conceptual framework most suitable to explain continental crossroads and the processes of its formations of culture and socio-spatial relations is that of translation. Translation here no longer stands as translating text A written in a language into text B written in another language. Translation, given its embedded premise of transfer and communication, on the contrary stands as a conceptual tool which can most plausibly conceptualise the nature of crossroads and help develop mechanisms that facilitates their survival as crossroads. Translation can also, therefore, explain why shared knowledge forms or shared significations of knowledge forms across diversity develop and perpetuate in crossroads. But in the process, the idea of translation too is widened, for it no longer remains a link or inter-relation between two texts, beginning from a source text and ending in a target text. Translation becomes a process through which the diverse participate to develop forms which are shared and which play a vital role in allowing the diversity to reproduce. Thus, from the diverse elements, through a process of translation, a shared element across the diversity is developed. In the last quarter of a century, one of the most significant contributions of South Asian studies on translation has been that the idea and practice of translation needs to step beyond the framework of relations between two given language per se. It is only then, as the classic three volume study of S.K. Das (1990-93) shows, that transcreation and language formation can be accommodated within the conceptual scope of translation. Genzler's recent study on *Translation and Identities in the Americas* (2008) seems to be an attempt at recognising the point at an international level.

But the existing South Asian studies have not taken into account the question of continental crossroads when discussing translation. The significant step taken in discussions of transcreations was that translation came to be seen as between one language and another language in the making, the latter making a transition from only oral into oral-written continuum form of language. However, in the case of continental crossroads and development of shared knowledge forms, translation no longer is transfer and communication of matter between languages, irrespective of the stage or nature of language formation process. Translation is how the diverse, through an active and participative process of transfer and communication, develops shared knowledge forms from the diverse as unique elements which the diverse also makes access to, to communicate among each other and but also to remain diverse.

We would conclude on the issue of translation as accommodation of diversity with another example from the valley, not to show how translation takes place from 'book' A to 'book' B but on the need to approach translation as beyond the notions of source text and target text itself. In 1981, Rong Bong Terong's classic novel *Rongmilir Hanhi* (The Smile of the Village Rongmili) was published. The novel was based on the life of the Karbi people who inhabit the Karbi hills to the south of the Brahmaputra valley. Situated in the early part of the 20th century, the novel maps the problem of land alienation in the hill in which the indigenous people were being displaced by migrants from the Gangetic delta of present day Bangladesh. The novel is considered an Assamese novel. But though the syntactic structure of language followed was that of modern Assamese, morphologically, the entire novel is bi-lingual. The Karbi community, like the Bodo or the Mising communities (as discussed earlier) constitute one of the communities of the trans-Brahmaputra valley and who use assamese as a shared practice in their everyday or social existence rather than as a structured language per se. In the present times, Karbi is considered a 'dialect'. One of the underlying questions that the novel poses is how does a 'dialect' communicate if communication (i.e. writing) is to be through a 'language'. Therefore, though the syntactic structure of modern Assamese is used, morphologically, the entire novel is kept bi-lingual. Karbi terms, names, forms of address, etc are used. These terms are explained in footnotes. The use of these terms were retained despite cases when availability of close equivalents in standard Assamese, such as for village head or wife, etc, being available. *Rongmilir Hanhi* was one of the most emphatic statements in modern Assamese literature on the question of Assamese, highlighting how even through written narratives, the relation between the dominant and the dominated (i.e. 'language' vs 'dialect') can be explored and commented upon. When the novel was published, there were massive civil movements in the valley (called Assam Agitation) on the issue of Assamese identity.

What is important about the novel for our discussion is that the novel is not merely a text, but a text which is also a critique of the modern practice of 'language'. The novel is not a rejection of 'language' or vice versa, but a statement on the dialectic between practices of communication, and problems of situating 'dialects' in such contemporary practices. Therefore, there is an active and critical communication between 'language' and 'dialect'. The method adopted to situate the critique within the text transformed it into text-in-translation. Throughout the novel there is a constant inter-play between 'dialect' and 'language' and how the only possible mode to create the Karbi everyday or social life in the narrative is to juxtapose 'language' and 'dialect'. Is it a case of language shift or the politics of language maintenance? But it could even more plausibly be a case of the struggle about the eroding dialectic of communication, one of the consequences as seen in the survey discussed before when communities aspire to but are unable to 'define' their celebration of spring. When seen in terms of the dialectic of communication, *Rongmilir Hanhi* could be argued to be conceptually based on the praxis of transfer and communication. The assumption of language as central to understanding of the narrative can only explain the political context of dominant vs dominated, i.e. the problem which is being attacked in the text. To explain the narrative form itself that constitutes the novel, more plausibly than language, it is the conceptual framework of translation and its premise of transfer and communication which could be considered more central.

Translating Culture Through Religion
The works of women *Bhakta* saints

Meeta Narain

The theme "Translation and the Accommodation of Diversity: Indian and non-Indian Perspectives", brings forth the multifaceted nature of translation studies. It speaks of the fact that diversity is an integral part of translation and it is through this diversity the lexical, textual, social, political and cultural aspects of the languages existing in different societies is portrayed. To quote Sarah Dudek in the article, 'Walter Benjamin & The Religion of Translation' in the Cipher Journal, *"A real translation is transparent; it does not cover the original, does not block its light, but allows the pure language, as though reinforced by its own medium, to shine upon the original all the more fully."*[1] The author further says in the article that, *"The particular languages are thus only incomplete pieces of the pure original. It is this idea which leads to the understanding of language as not only a communicative tool between humans, but moreover the realm of hidden divine truth, of something enigmatic which is totally free of meaning and resonating in the human languages. Benjamin builds his teleology on the basis of this mystical idea: the final aim is to approach divine language, in which all truth is hidden, but which is at the same time no longer communicative, but rather totally free of meaning. Translation is the decisive means to reach the final end: it completes languages, puts together the disintegrated "modes of intention"—as Benjamin calls the sphere in semiotics termed "signifier"—and works towards the perfection of the original, which can be considered incomplete, requiring translation: "Thus translation, ironically, transplants the original into a more definitive linguistic realm", Benjamin states.*[2]

In today's globalised world, cultural diversity through translations is being promoted. Foreign literature-be it classical, theoretical or religious is experiencing new heights in the field of translation. The cultural diversity is being promoted through translations. Translation brings closer the fragmentation of human culture and meaning. What is alien and different can be made familiar and comprehensible.

It is in view of this that translation studies today are bringing in ideas from the fields of not only politics and economics but also from sociology, anthropology and religious studies of one language and society into another. Religious documents are being translated in a big way and a deep interest in it is being observed. Religion, as an important aspect of society, portrays the cultural growth of a society and in this perspective, translating culture through religion plays a dominant role. Religion can be viewed from different aspects, and one of it is the medieval period and its translations. The following paper being innovative in nature takes into account the works of women bhakta saints and the need and importance of their translations.

In today's era of globalization, religion and its manifestations such as socio-cultural movements, oral traditions and textual works by leading saints have come to occupy a distinctive place in the cultural development of societies. They are essential tools for all fields of development – political, cultural and social, extending religion beyond the purview of worship onto functional aspects of living. Translating religion and religious documents are today an integral part of the culture of any society since they not only acquaint the reader with the prevalent world religions but also address several unanswered questions in difficult times.

The culture of any country is shaped by its long history, unique geography, diverse demographics and the absorption of customs, traditions and ideas from sources such as its neighbours and the preservation of ancient heritages, which are formed on the basis of the by-gone years. What makes a culture different from the others is not the way it expresses ideas but the way it analyses experience. As has been expressed by Jamal Eddine Benhayoun in his book, Translating Culture: The Economy of Articulation and Confinement, *"Culture is a key concept that is capable of re-inventing itself as a history of culture itself. Our contemporaries, our postmodernism and post-colonialism seem to be entrapped within the very word we naively think we master. The trends of our thinking, the turns in our cultural and ideological attitudes, our modernity and post-modernity, our current cultural practices are all homogenized and simplified, within the word culture"*[3]. And to translate this simplified, yet sophisticated form of culture is indeed a challenge before the translator since, the translation, as we all would agree, is not only a linguistic substitution of the lexis but a total cultural transformation. The role of the translator, is therefore, to facilitate the transfer of message, meaning and cultural elements from one language into another and create an equivalent response from the receivers. The source language carries the essence of the cultural context which has to be transferred to the target language.

The great diversity of religious practices, languages, customs, and traditions are examples of a unique co-mingling of different aspects of culture, which, each in their own manner, influence other parts of the world. In India, religion is a way of life. It is an integral part of the entire Indian tradition. For the majority of Indians, religion permeates every aspect of life, from common-place daily chores to education and politics.

As a cultural bedrock, India has been well known as the originator of several religious practices. Its diversified systems of faith, languages, customs and traditions have co-mingled to produce a vibrant cultural pattern. This variegated socio cultural fabric has found points of identification for people from all over the world, hence allowing them to relate to multiple spiritual aspects. Evidence of a global response to these spiritual systems have exceeded purely religious definitions, and have been seen in the cultural practices such as art, music and theatre that have evolved in different parts of the world. In Times Online dated 6th April 2010, filed under "Faith and Culture" it has been said, and I quote *"Artists responded to religious commissions with some of their finest works. And it was not just money that moved them. They worked in the service of a faith that could lift their talents above the level of mere illustration and offer a supreme test of skill."* Further, *"Culture often takes the role of religion in our contemporary world. Galleries are modern-day temples, regularly attended by the people on their day of rest".*[4]

The author also discusses the fact that *"irreverent subversion"* of religion in art only indicates a form of paying homage to the power of religion. He says, *"on the flipside of their blasphemies lies the acknowledgement of the potency of the symbols they attack"*[5]. Hence, the varied artistic critiques of mainstream religion merging Eastern and Western thought can be seen as an alternative way of communication. And I quote again, *"In their means of expression they herald and witness hope for humanity, dispel the fear of approaching the first and last source of beauty and enter into dialogue with believers. Faith takes nothing away from your genius or your art. On the contrary it exalts them and nourishes them"*[6]. As such the interest in religious movements is now becoming a universal factor of interests for people from all walks of life.

Taking the case of India, Hinduism as the dominant faith exists in a larger milieu of religious diversity, with some of the most deeply religious societies and cultures embedded within it. Religion plays a central and definitive role in the lives of its people, and has traveled across its boundaries to influence people from other parts of the world too. Critiques of Hinduism have originated in artistic and linguistic realms from both within and outside India. Spiritual systems rooted in India have traveled globally, and one of the lesser known migrants has been of Bhakti philosophy. The Bhakti saints were one such community that questioned prevailing Brahminical religious orders, and through their art and poetry depicted the defiance of the rules, regulations or societal ordering.

A niche interest in this larger purview is the significant role of women Bhakta Saints in developing a system of faith accessible to the masses. Hence, it is imperative to consider the philosophical contributions of women Bhakta saints from India who redefined concepts of gender, language and devotion and established a spiritual legacy vibrant even today. The same is directly made visible in the processes of translation. Keeping this in view, the works of women Bhakta saints stand out prominently as alternatives to extant ways of thought and living.

Translated works of saints such as Akkamahadevi, Janabai, Mirabai, Bahinabai and others are a beacon to guide women across nations in times of political and personal turmoil, providing them with succor and strength. The presence of translated works of saints such as the above in foreign languages specially in the Russian language offers a fertile ground to examine the spiritual mindset of a people in a time of change. And to translate these religious aspects so as to portray the cultural development of the nation is a challenge before the translator, since translation is not only a linguistic transformation from one language to another but a cultural transference of one heritage from one language of thought to another.

The variegated roles played by women Bhakta saints, including their roles as revolutionary Bhakta saints, as domestic but liberated literary figures and as central contributors to an unprecedented spiritual movement in India lend them a significant space in the country's religious history. Women Bhakta saints in their lives as maverick individuals set example for the defiance of social norms in the face of devotional passion, as reflected in their unconventional usage of ordinary language and alternative systems of worship. This paper investigates the extent to which women across nationalities gain from cultural readings of the lives of women Bhakta saints from India. The impact of the philosophy of women Bhakta saints is palpable through the available translations of their works in foreign languages. Russian translations of the same in a changing society draw the interest of a cross section of the public today.

Being an academic of Russian language and translation, I can evidence the interest in Indian religious philosophy in post 1991 Russia. There is growing inquisitiveness among the public to be acquainted with the various religious movements and follow the paths of Hindu mythology and saints. This has resulted in scholars visiting India and vice versa, who are promoting religious culture through translations.

After the disintegration of the Soviet Union the Russian society opened to international cultural influences. The resultant changes that have taken place portray a dramatic period in the history of the country, arising from the confluence of multi faceted cultural forces. Against this backdrop, translations of works of revolutionary women Bhakta saints are gaining popularity amidst the transmutating perspectives of the Russian public. Challenges have arisen in the context of linguistic technicalities, since the vocabulary today is full of novel terminologies which the translators have to contend with so as to remain truthful to literary content. The challenges of historicization arise when translations require capturing the cultural and religious nuances of bygone periods, further enhanced by local colloquial transformations through time. Women Bhakta Saints uniquely evolved oral and literary traditions in opposition to classicized linguistic patterns, requiring specialized knowledge to translate them accurately today. To understand this format the translator needs in depth cultural knowledge in addition to linguistic skills, presenting a novel dimension of possible inter-cultural translational exchange.

Keeping these phenomena in mind, this paper has tried to widen its purview by not only discussing the translations of specific literary aspects of women Bhakta saints such as Meerabai, Janabai, Akkamahadevi, Bahinabai and others, but also investigates their feminine power and its subsequent socio cultural impact on the Russian society. While some texts by women saints have been translated into Russian in a directly literary way, further widening of the very concept of 'translation' can reveal holistic knowledge of the associated cultural system. For instance, their roles as revolutionary leaders, users of simplified language, or challenging the patriarchal system and so on, empowering them, need to yet be translated in order to perceive the socio cultural impacts on society.

Similar works have been likewise translated into several European languages, to illustrate the integration of culture and spiritual thought. The thrust of the argument of this paper has entailed the political, personal and sexual alternatives that Bhakti philosophy by women saints proposed to the social milieu for all times to come. In time of personal and political crisis as nations undergo tumultuous change, spirituality is considered to offer succor and strength, and this paper has engaged in the transference of belief systems of knowledge from women of one age to another, crossing the borders of time, space and language.

The novel and revolutionary nature of Bhakti traditions in oral and written form incited Russian and Indian scholars to investigate and translate them, such that they are made accessible to the masses. Sites with translations by AK Ramanujan are one of the most popular translations into English. *A.K. Ramanujan's* collections contain essays, *"On Women Saints"*, which are a valuable analysis of the similarities and differences among the lives of the women saints of India, and have thus been translated into other Indian and foreign languages.

Of similar importance are translations done by Vijaya Ramaswamy – a scholar from south whose study includes translations of several poems on women, society and spirituality. Armando Menezes and S. M. Angadi who have translated 315 poems by Akka Mahadevi are also popular names in the field of translation on women bhakta saints. In Russian sites are available, where we find translations done by scholars like;

Воробьева, Марина В., Иваненко, Сергей Игоревич, Альбедиль, М. Ф. Иванова, Л. В., Иваненко, Сергей Игоревич, Гусева, Н. Р. of books and verses. The popularity of sacred books such as the Srimad Bhagvad and publications of movements led by saints such as those of ISKCON in Russian are a few outstanding examples in the field of translation.

Amongst the most popular works which have been translated into Russian language, are those of Mirabai, a high caste north Indian woman Bhakta saint. Translations of her life and works can be highlighted in four categories: her biography that speaks of her unique life as a saint and poetess; her life after marriage into a wealthy family and the manner in which it was distinguished from her childhood; her role as a social reformer who refused to immolate herself through the practice of sati and challenged patriarchy; and her role as a revolutionary saint who sought to establish alternative social orders through life examples. Events in her life stand as testimony of her existence as a feminist, activist and spiritual leader amalgamated into one personality. This multifaceted character has enamored western societies today, who look at her life for inspiration as much as her verses for their essence. A translation from *"The Life of Mirabai"* by Swami Shivananda in Russian speaks of the above mentioned qualities Meera in the following manner (*Чрезвычайно трудно найти параллель замечательной личности Миры – святой, поэтессы и мудрой женщины. Её жизнь была уникальным, единственным явлением, олицетворяющим необычную красоту и чудо. Она была принцессой, но отказалась от удовольствий и роскоши, свойственных её высокому положению. Вместо этого она выбрала бедную, аскетическую и бесстрастную жизнь. Несмотря на то, что она была нежной молодой женщиной, она отправилась в опасное путешествие по духовному пути и подверглась различным суровым испытаниям с неустрашимой храбростью. Она обладала гигантской волей*).[7] It is pertinent to say here, that the original surrounding cultural context or socio historic ethos of any text must be preserved in its translations. Verses when accompanied by biographic descriptions of the saint help to gauge her socio historical identity and translations of the same portray her unique identity, as mentioned in the English version of the same text by AJ Alston in the book titled *The devotional poems of Mirabai* (1980): "*It is extremely difficult to find a parallel to this wonderful personality –Mira-a saint, a philosopher, a poet and a sage. She was a versatile genius and a magnanimous soul. Her life has a singular charm, with extraordinary beauty and marvel.*"[8] Such translated texts then open up for a comprehensive materialist reading, especially in the feminist domain, as evident in the Russian perspective after the perestroika.

The great amount of interest in the latter has been exemplified by the fact that where translations do not or cannot exist, there exist transliterations of her verses. These are accompanied by explanatory sentences, to help foreign audiences comprehend their meaning. To explain this point I quote from one of the articles entitled, 'Life of Mirabai (in Russian) – by Saipriya Vishwanathan says *"Мере Ту Гиридхар Гопал Доосро На Кои"* *"Только Гиридхар Гопал важен для меня, никто иной"*.[9]

Often simplicity in comprehension is facilitated by the presence of conventional spellings which suggest socio cultural meanings and pose a challenge to translation. The woman saint Akkamahadevi in the 12th century used extraordinarily simplified and plebian language for her poetry where she uses words such as *maya*, *samsara*, which have proliferate meaning in the local context, which although difficult to capture in a foreign language are the very words that explicate the personalities and social context of the original author. A dominant feature of the Bhakti movement was the women writing in their own local languages which made devotion and prayer accessible to every member of society, including lower caste Hindus and untouchables. Poetry when written in local languages such as by Akkamahadevi was a rejection of Sanskritist superiority and exclusive knowledge of the scriptures. She was a Bhakta from the southern region of Karnataka and belonged to a lower caste within the Hindu fold. She attracted large audiences to include the marignalised segments of Hindu society such as women and untouchables, since her poetry was locally understood by all. She was a wandering minstrel who discarded social conventions and marks of feminine identity, which raised eyebrows among men and challenged her devotion. To elucidate the above point regarding contexts and difficulties in translation is one of Akkamahadevi's verses, making several oblique references to local, geographical and natural elements. These internally bear much meaning to be understood by the resident public, and equally difficult to accurately translate and explain to a foreign one. In A K Ramanujan's translation, the verse reads:

> *Would a circling surface vulture know*
> *such depths of sky as the moon would know?*
> *would a weed on the riverbank*
> *know such depths of water*
> *as the lotus would know?*
> *would a fly darting nearby*
> *know the smell of flowers*
> *as the bee would know?*
> *O lord white as jasmine*
> *only you would know*
> *the way of your devotees:*
> *how would these,*
> *these*
> *mosquitoes*
> *on the buffalo's hide?*[10]

These references to central and peripheral elements of nature speak of Akkamahadevi's status as an untouchable, in the periphery of the caste system, to who worship was not as accessible as the higher echelons of the caste order. Yet, in these examples, the proximity to the centre is explicated through devotion, such as the bee to the flower as compared to the passing fly such that Bhakti or devotion stands above caste differences. It may be questioned whether to understand these relationships between elements of the natural kingdom in the local setting of the Kannada landscape, accurate translations of not only words but entire contexts are possible? This concern extends further when there is a three way translation between regional language, English and then the foreign language. Scholars equally adept in all three in order to preserve the essence of the text are very rare.

The poetry of Janabai, a 13th century woman Bhakta saint emerged in medieval India when the forces of caste were strong, and considered an obstacle in the path of devotion. She belonged to a low caste Shudra family but was sent to the home of Namdev, an uppercaste Bhakta saint, where she was converted to a devotee in addition to her household chores. Her sensitive poetry which is popular even today illuminates the everyday life of ordinary lives of ordinary women and addresses its joys and strains. In her poetry she is intensely aware of her position in society as a servant girl, and inspired by Namdev's poetry, speaks of her hopes to discard all social conventions or bonds of respectability, so that nothing stands between her and her beloved Vithoba or Krishna. She wrote:

> *"Let me not be sad because I am born a woman*
> *In this world, many saints suffer this way"*[11]
> (translated from Marathi by Vilas Sarang)

Passages from Janabai's biography reflect the socio cultural milieu of her times. Translating one such segment into Russian, which would address the central issue of this paper concerning inter language exchange is a hard task for the translator. Taking an example from a translation by Anjali Yardi reads as follows:

> *When Jani sweeps the floor*
> *her Lord gathers up the dirt.*
> *When she lifts the wooden pestle*
> *he cleans the mortar stone.*
> *He doesn't stand on dignity*
> *he collects cow-pats* by her side.*
> *When she goes to fetch the water*
> *her Lord follows after.*[12]

Translating such simple lines and passages into Russian pose a difficulty because without understanding the background and psychology of such deep yet simple *Bhaktas*, it is impossible to attempt translating such a piece.

Mary McGee in her book titled "*Bahinabai: the ordinary life of an exceptional woman*"[13] sets an example of a Saint from within the domestic fold who followed her spiritual calling while also keeping to her womanly duties as a wife. She was a poet saint from 17th century Maharashtra and wrote *abangas* or women's songs that accompanied their labours, especially in the fields. She had duty and respectful empathy towards both her marriage and her spouse, as reflected in her poetry. Despite being a high caste woman, she was a devotee of the low caste poet Tukaram, choosing the path of devotion over brahminical norms of ritual purity. She wrote *abanga* verse which depicted relevant social practices and her responses to it, highlighting the potency of her thoughts. The translation of her *abangas* are available in the book on Bahinabai titled, '*A Translation of Autobiography and Verses*' by Justin E. Abbot[14], which have the need to be translated to show the socio cultural impact on the society. The works of saints such as Janabai, Bahinabai and others except Meerabai are, as far as I know, unavailable in Russian language and seek space in Russian literature.

The essential importance of translation of lives and works of women Bhakta saints into Russian speaks of the fact that while battling with extant social structures they were monumental figures in the same. They struggled to reconcile the tensions of social expectation from them as women and householders, with their own unique devotional inspiration and conviction. The present world takes inspiration from the life stories of these saints whose lives while being locally specific were also universally understood. The central significance of examining this field is for today's generation to understand the grand reverence for women over centuries, in spite of all odds against them. Hence the translation of such descriptions are not mere 'documents' to be preserved, but as Susie Tharu has said, in her book women writings in India, "*are documents that display what is at stake in the embattled practices of self and agency, and in the making of a habitable world, at the margins of patriarchies reconstituted by the emerging bourgeoisies of empire and nation.*"[15]

Russia in the post perestroika period witnesses the phenomenon of religious movement accompanied by varied literary strains including religious literature of the east and the west. This literature, including Hindu texts in their different aspects has had an impact on the language, culture and civilization of the people. Translated works of women saints can be read at par with mainstream literature in order to gauge a conventional set of meanings, in conjunction with class, nation, gender and so on. However, writings of women Bhakta Saints are in fact gestures of implicit defiance of subversion, not only moments in which they collude with or reinforce dominant ideologies of gender, class, nation or empire. The Russian reception of works on and by Meerabai indicates the keenness of the west in this field, opening the doors for future translations of works by other women Bhakta Saints. These possible works shall hope to focus on the multi faceted roles played by the women Bhakta saints, whose impact on the medieval and contemporary society gives new meaning to the rich cultures of other countries.

Bibliography

1. Sarah Dudek, Walter Benjamin & The Religion of Translation, http://www.cipherjournal.com/html/dudek_benjamin.html.
2. Ibid.
3. Jamal Eddine Benhayoun, Translating Culture: The Economy of Articulation and Confinement' (Abdelmalek Essaadi University, Tetuan, Morocco) http://www.scholars.nus.edu.sg/post/poldiscourse/casablanca/benhayoun1.html.
4. Let's get artists into our churches – Times Online (London), April 2, 2010, by Rachel Campbell Johnston: http://entertainment.timesonline.co.uk/tol/arts_and_entertainment/visual_arts/article7084421.ece.
5. Ibid.
6. Ibid.
7. Swami Shivananda, *Life of Mirabai*, http://www.kulichki.com/~yoga/ Shivananda/Bhakti/bhakti1505.htm.
8. Alston A.J., *The Devotional Poems of Mirabai*, Asian Humanities Press, Delhi, 1980.
9. Vishwanathan S., *Life of Mirabai (in Russian)*, http://sai.org.ua/ru/152.html.
10. Ramanujan A.K., *Speaking of Siva*, (The Penguin classics). Harmondsworth, Penguin, 1973.
11. Tharu S. and Lalita K., *Women Writing in India,* Vol. 1, Oxford University Press, New Delhi 1991, Pg. 82.
12. Yardi Anjali, http://www.shadowtrain.com/shadowtrain/id108.html.
13. *Source:* McGee, Mary. "Bahinabai: The Ordinary Life of an Exceptional Woman, or, the Exceptional Life of an Ordinary Woman." In *Vaisnavi: Women and the Worship of Krishna.* Edited by Steven J. Rosen. Delhi: Motilal Banarsidass, 1996. on the website: http://chnm.gmu.edu/wwh/modules/lesson1/lesson1.php?s=8.
14. Abbot, J. E. *A Translation of Autobiography and Verses*, Pune Scottish Mission Industries, 1929.
15. Tharu S. and Lalita K., *Women Writing in India,* Vol. 1, Oxford University Press, New Delhi 1991, Pg. 36.

Translating Indian Language Proverbs: What do they Contribute to Translation Theory?

Panchanan Mohanty

Proverbs are brief, pithy and semi-frozen texts that express the collective wisdom of a speech-community. These are introduced in a conversation to serve definite purposes and are, to a great extent, specific to the language, the society and the culture in which they are used. But proverbs belong to a dying genre in the sense that the younger generation speakers, in general, use them much less frequently than their elders. Then, though translations of proverbs from one language to another are found, there is hardly any theoretical discussion available on this subject. All these make translation of proverbs a challenging and significant interdisciplinary area of study, especially in the Indian context simply because of the diverse and complex linguistic, social, and cultural scenario of the subcontinent. It need not be emphasized that the most important aspect of a proverb is its meaning, and in order to understand the meaning of a proverb it is necessary to know both the denotations as well as the connotations of the words that constitute it. As Firth (1926:134) pointed out long ago: "The meaning of a proverb is made clear only when side by side with the translation is given a full account of the accompanying social situation- the reason for its use, its effect, and its significance in speech." Indian languages and cultures, which belong to at least four different streams, i.e. Indo-Aryan, Dravidian, Munda and Tibeto-Burman, have been in close contact for millennia, and it has led to a deep convergence at the linguistic and cultural levels among them. As a result, each one of them possesses a large number of words that originally belong to the other three genetic stocks. But lexicography is not a very developed field of study in modern India. There is hardly any dictionary dealing with two Indian languages barring Hindi even today. So it is not surprising that Indian language lexicographers are not fully aware of the sources of most of the words mentioned above and, therefore, these words are swept under the category of *deshi* or native by them.

Interestingly, we find many proverbs in Indian languages that contain these so-called *deshi* or native words. Sometimes such words are used only in the proverbs and nowhere else in the concerned language, and there is hardly any discussion on this issue in the literature on proverbs. On the one hand, most Indian language dictionaries do not give proper and adequate information about these borrowed and assimilated words, and that is why, it is difficult to determine their meanings in the relevant contexts. On the other hand, even if the experienced speakers of a language are able to interpret these proverbs correctly, they cannot always give the meaning of each of its constituent words. Hence, these tiny texts create a real problem for translation.

Keeping these in view, I will focus in this paper on certain proverbs from Oriya, a major Indo-Aryan language spoken in the eastern Indian state of Orissa, to demonstrate the issues and problems outlined above. In fact, the key words employed in these Oriya proverbs have been either misrepresented semantically or completely ignored in the existing Oriya dictionaries. I intend to show here that an appropriate translation of these proverbs crucially depends on determining the meanings of these words. And for achieving this, one must first understand the diversity in the linguistic and cultural scenario of India. In other words, a translator must be familiar with the neighbouring languages and cultures, especially those belonging to the other genetic stocks and those which are supposed to have been in close contact for centuries.

1. Introduction

I have heard the following two proverbs in my childhood in a remote village of Orissa, an eastern state of the Indian subcontinent quite frequently, especially from the mouth of the womenfolk including my mother and other female members in the family:

1. a:paNa: suna: bheNDi
   own gold lady's finger/okra
   'My own gold is lady's finger/okra.'
2. ka:Li kotari, hĕsa muturi
   black ____ , big grass reed mat urinating
   '(She is) dark complexioned and wets the big grass reed mat."

No gloss is given for /kotari/ because this word does not find a place as a headword in any Oriya dictionary published so far. Although I fully understood the meaning of these two proverbs, their semantic non-compositionality was intriguing. To be specific, these two words, i.e. /bheNDi/ in (1) and /kotari/ in (2) along with the following questions have bothered me for years:

a) What is the relation between /suna:/, the expensive and precious metal 'gold' and /bheNDi/, the ordinary and common vegetable 'lady's finger/okra'?
b) What might have been the motivation for the Oriya lexicographers not to consider /kotari/ as a headword?

Now I have found more convincing answers for both these questions, and that is what I intend to discuss in this paper.

2. What is /bheNDi/?

/bheNDi/ is a name widely used in most parts of India to designate a green vegetable called 'lady's finger/okra' in English. So it is natural that all Oriya lexicographers have given the same as the only meaning for this word (Dash 1971:921, Nanda Sharma 2008:813, Padhi 2008:921). But some others have given a second meaning along with this one. For example, Praharaj (1936:6144) has added the following meanings: (i) gold of inferior quality, (ii) gold adulterated with baser metal, an alloy of gold, and (iii) a gilt metal. It should be noted that Praharaj's seven-volume *pu:rNacandra oDia: bha:Sa:koSa*, published originally between 1931 and 1940, is the first exhaustive and encyclopedic Oriya dictionary that has remained unparalleled even today. Therefore, many later lexicographers have followed it while compiling their dictionaries. But they have rejected the second meaning 'alloyed/adulterated gold' for /bheNDi/. The reason is obvious. The above cited proverb is the only example for this meaning of /bheNDi/ in Oriya. It is certainly a highly marked situation which is not noticed in languages of the world. On the other hand, it is almost impossible to establish a semantically compatible link between gold and lady's finger/okra. This is what made me quite uncomfortable about this proverb and I started looking for a more convincing alternative

The proverb /a:pana: suna: bheNDi/ is normally used in the following context: Imagine a situation when a son, who is supposed to look after his parents in their old age, does not do it. That is when the parents use this proverb. Thus, it means "My gold is not gold. (It is some other lesser metal)." During my search for an alternative meaning of /bheNDi/, I discovered that Telugu has a word /weNDi/ 'silver' (*SSN*:427), and it perfectly suits the interpretation of the proverb, i.e. 'My gold is not pure gold; it is silver, a lesser metal.' It is also quite natural for /weNDi/ to become /bheNDi/ in the Oriya speech because barring a handful of words (e.g. /bewa:/ 'a widow', /ha:wa:/ 'wind') most of which are borrowed lately from other languages, /w/ does not occur independently in Oriya. It, of course, occurs in consonant clusters especially in words borrowed from Sanskrit, e.g. /kwacit/ 'hardly', /pakwa/ 'ripe', etc. In other environments, it is realised as /b/, e.g. /warša/ 'year', /wasanta/ 'the spring season' have become /barsa/ and /basanta/. It will not be out of place to mention that the Oriya alphabet did not have a separate letter for /w/ until the 20th century, and the newly invented letter for /w/ is very strange because it consists of the letter for the vowel /o/ with the

113

allograph of /w/ below it. However, it is quite possible that the Dravidian word /weNDi/ first became /beNDi/ in Oriya; but the Oriya speech community forgot its meaning over a period of time as the concerned proverb contained the sole occurrence of this word conveying the meaning 'silver'. Then, they did not know how to interpret it. The phonologically closest word available in Oriya was /bheNDi/ 'lady's finger/okra', and, as a result, the Oriya speakers transformed it to /bheNDi/. Such changes are referred to as 'folk etymology' in historical linguistics and these are quite normal in the history of human languages. Let us take a few examples from English. The Old English 'sam-blind' (semi- or half-blind) became 'sand-blind' in the Elizabethan period (Bloomfield 1963:423). Again, the French word 'sur-loin' that contains 'sur' derived from Latin 'super' has changed to 'sir-loin' in English (Lehmann 1976:187). These examples clearly demonstrate that whenever a word in a larger construction becomes semantically opaque, the speakers tend to replace it by a closely related word available to them in order to make its meaning transparent. Most probably, the change of /weNDi/ to /bheNDi/ has gone through the same process.

3. The mysterious /kotari/

As mentioned above, /kotari/ has not been listed as a headword in any Oriya dictionary published so far. As proverb (1) is the only instance in Oriya that contains /bheNDi/ in the sense of 'silver', proverb (2) cited above is the only Oriya expression in which /kotari/ occurs as a noun. Of course, there is a dialectal /kotari/ denoting a small sized fresh water fish in the western variety of Oriya that is called kera:NDi (Tripathy 1987:74) whose zoological name is 'Barbus chola'. Though it is also a noun, I have not considered it here simply because it has been borrowed into western Oriya from the language(s) spoken in the contiguous Bastar area of the state of Chhattisgarh (Deb 1976:616). Therefore, the above mentioned single occurrence of /kotari/ as a noun in the whole Oriya language corpus may be the cause of its non-inclusion in the existing Oriya dictionaries. But a phonetically similar adjective /kotara:/ is found in almost all Oriya dictionaries, and its synonyms are 'dirty, nasty, foul, soiled, worn out'. Deb (1976:616) has given two nominal equivalents /maiLa:/ and /maLi/ meaning 'dirt' for this word. But this nominal usage is so very marked that I have never encountered it in Oriya, either in speech or in writing, until today and other Oriya speakers also find it odd. For this reason, /kotara:/ should better be treated as an adjective in Oriya and I will do the same in this paper.

However, coming back to our focal point, only Praharaj (1932:1794) and *OBK* (1998:749) have mentioned /kotari/ as the feminine from of /kotara:/. It is not at all convincing because the proverb /ka:Li kotari, hẽsa muturi/ starts with the adjective /ka:Li/ 'black' followed by /kotari/. If we accept the adjectival synonyms of /kotari/ given above and translate the expression as 'black dirty', 'black nasty', 'black foul', 'black soiled', 'black worn out', we will end up with unacceptable expressions. On the other hand, the remaining part of the proverb, i.e. /hẽsa muturi/ 'urinating on big grass reed mat' clearly implies that /kotari/ is a person who sleeps on a big mat made of grass reed and wets it. Again, the modifiers /ka:Li/ 'black, dark complexioned (fem.)' and /muturi/ 'urinating, wetting (fem.)' make it evident that the person is a woman.

All these pieces of information along with a very strong Dravidian substratum in Orissa reflected in the place-names and cultural practices (Mohanty 2002, 2003, 2008) as well as the presence of innumerable Dravidian words in the Oriya language make it almost certain that the Telugu word /ku:turu/ denoting 'girl, daughter' (*SSN*:340) is the source of /kotari/ in the Oriya proverb under discussion. If this is accepted, then the meaning of this proverb will be: 'The girl is dark-complexioned and she wets bed (at night).' Thus, the implication is that she is not a good match for marriage. In fact, this is the context in which this proverb is normally used. It will not be out of place to point out that /peLLi ku:turu/, literally meaning 'marriage girl' or 'bride' (*SSN*: 349), is a very frequently and widely used collocation in Telugu, the dominant language of the state of Andhra Pradesh that is the immediate southern neighbour of Orissa. Substitution of the word-final /u/ by /i/ in Oriya /kotari/ has most likely been carried out for two reasons: (i) to make it conform to the Oriya feminine forms that end in /i/, e.g. /Toki/ 'lass', /buDhi/ 'old woman', /pa:gaLi/ 'mad (fem.)' and (ii) to make it rhyme with /muturi/ 'urinating' that occurs in the second part of the proverb. Notice that all the three consonants of the Telugu word, i.e. /k, t, r/ have been retained in Oriya whereas the remaining two vowels, i.e. /u:/ and /u/ have changed to /o/ and /a/ respectively. So these changes have to be accounted for in order to support our argument. I have argued elsewhere that dialects, not standard languages, are more stable and reliable repositories of the borrowings from other languages (Mohanty 2008). The presence of /hẽsa/ 'big grass reed mat', a word used mostly by the rural folks and the subaltern, and the context in which this proverb is normally employed make it evident that it represents a non-standard, dialectal culture. In other words, my contention is that the proverb under discussion most probably originated in dialectal Oriya and at a later stage got into Standard Oriya through the process of assimilation that includes the necessary phonological changes. Interestingly, the northern Oriya dialect uses

/kuturi/ for /kotari/ in this proverb even today. So its northern Oriya variant is: /ka:Li kuturi, hẽsa muturi/.

It is worth mentioning here that articulation on /u/ is generally considered dialectal and sub-standard by the Standard Oriya speakers just because /o/ in a number of Standard Oriya words is found to have been substituted by /u/ in certain dialects as well as in rural and low caste speech. For example:

Standard Oriya	Dialectal Oriya	Gloss
oda:	uda: (N.O., W.O.)	wet
osa:	usa: (N.O.)	a religious fast or vow
oTara:	uTura: (N.O., L.C.O.)	dragging, pulling
oDasa	uDusa (N.O., W.O., L.C.O.)	bed-bug
oDhaNa:	uDhuNa: (N.O.)	veil
koThi	kuThi (N.O., W.O.)	building, room
koLatha	kuLutha (N.O., W.O., L.C.O.)	horse gram
koraDa:	kuruDa: (N.O.)	whip, scourge
koraNa:	kuruNa: (N.O., L.C.O.)	scraper
khora:k	khura:k (N.O., L.C.O.)	food
khoLapa:	khuLupa: (N.O., L.C.O.)	outer covering
gokhara	gukhura (N.O., L.C.O.)	cobra
ghoDaNi	ghuDuNi (N.O.)	lid, cover
thoDi	thuDi (N.O., L.C.O.)	chin
pokara:	pukura: (N.O., L.C.O.)	worm-eaten
pokhari	pukhuri (N.O.)	tank, pond
phoTaka:	phuTuka: (N.O., W.O., L.C.O.)	bubble, blister
phoDaNi	phuDuNi (N.O.)	perforator
boka:	buka: (N.O.)	fool
boda:	buda: (N.O., W.O.)	billy goat
modaka	muduka (N.O., L.C.O.)	a traditional medicine rolled into small balls

As a result, a number of words whose sources possess /u/ show the same vowel in the dialects whereas it has been hypercorrected to /o/ in Standard Oriya. For example:

Dialectal Oriya	Source	Standard Oriya	Gloss
upara	upara (Skt.)	opara	above
upa:sa	upaba:sa (Skt.)	opa:sa	fasting
upa:Diba:	utpa:T- (Skt.)	opa:Diba:	to uproot
duka:na	duka:n (Arabic)	doka:na	shop
tuphan(a)	tufa:n (Persian)	topha:n(a)	tempest, hurricane

All these examples provide ample evidence that it is quite natural for the dialectal/ kuturi/ to become /kotari/ in Standard Oriya.

Now the question is whether /kotari/ is derived from /kotara:/. It is a general tendency in the world's languages to derive the feminine forms from their masculine counterparts, and the same is true in Oriya. Further, /kotari/ in the said proverb is a noun as it denotes a girl, whereas /kotara:/ is always used as an adjective and never as a noun in Oriya. Therefore, the adjective /kotara:/ cannot be the source of the noun /kotari/. Of course, the adjective /kotari/ can be derived from /kotara:/ by adding the feminine suffix /-i/; but it does not seem to be related to the noun /kotari/ in the proverb under consideration. So we can accept both the noun and the adjective /kotari/ as homonyms.

4. Amnesia in Oriya Society

When I started discovering a number of common words, place-names, and cultural practices originally belonging to Dravidian in Oriya and Orissa, some of my Oriya-speaking friends colleagues tried to dissuade me from doing this kind of research. Needless to say that it is symptomatic of an apathetic attitude of the Oriya elite towards all those features in the Oriya language and culture that are non-Aryan. The obvious fallout of it is that these non-Aryan elements have been sanitized in two ways: (i) by giving them an Aryan coating and (ii) by completely side-lining and ignoring them. As a result, they have been obliterated leading to amnesia in the Oriya society. Portraying the Munda tribal god Jagannath of Puri as Vishnu, the most important member of the Hindu trinity and inventing Sanskritic roots for the Dravidian words used in Oriya provide evidence for all these. For instance, Sanskrit /atyadbhuta/, which is a combination of two morphemes /ati+adbhuta/, has been determined to be the source of Oriya /aca:bhua:/ whose first occurrence is found in *sa:raLa: maha:bha:rata* of 15th century. From the context in which it has been used[2], one can easily make out that its equivalents should be 'frightened, bewildered' which are very different from the meaning of Sanskrit /atyadbhuta/ 'very strange'. Interestingly, earlier Oriya lexicographers (e.g. Praharaj 1931/2008:126) have mentioned it as a *deshaja* or native word whereas later scholars have treated it as a *tadbhava* word derived from Sanskrit (Mohapatra 1976:91). If we accept the latter view, then it is natural for /adbhuta/ to become */abhua:/; but interestingly no such word is has ever occurred in Oriya. Further, at least some other Sanskrit words containing /atya-/ should have changed to /acca-/ or /aca-/. For instance, /atyanta/ 'excessive' and /atyadhika/ 'very much' should have become */ac(c)anta/ and */ac(c)adhika/ respectively.

117

But these words are never found in Oriya. That is why, we can argue that Sanskrit /atyadbhuta/ is not the source of Oriya /aca:bhua:/. Hence, I had to look for its source elsewhere, and I found it in Dravidian. To be specific, Tamil has a word /acappu/ meaning 'inattentiveness', 'absence of mind' and another word /acaivu/ meaning 'weariness' and 'exhaustion' (Burrow and Emeneau 1984:5) that can be determined as the source of the concerned Oriya word from both the phonological as well as semantic points of view.

5. Conclusion

To conclude, I have considered in this paper two Oriya proverbs which are frequently used by the Oriya womenfolk and each one of them contains an extremely rare and fascinating word, such as /bheNDi/ and /kotari/. These two words have been either misinterpreted or ignored by the Oriya lexicographers. I have tried to provide an alternative interpretation for the word /bheNDi/ that is more appropriate than the earlier one in the context of the overall meaning of the proverb. The second proverb employs /kotari/ as a noun and it denotes a 'young woman'; but none of the Oriya lexicographers has given this meaning in their dictionaries. On the other hand, they have treated /kotari/ as a feminine form of the adjective /kotara:/. Needless to say that such a meaning is inappropriate in the present context and for this reason, I have preferred to link it to the Telugu word /ku:turu/ 'girl, daughter'. Finally, the implications of this study are twofold: a) As proverbs are semi-frozen expressions, any occurrence of a rare and strange word in them must be dealt with a lot of care and open-mindedness because it may hold the key to a hitherto unknown chapter in the life of the concerned language. b) Unlike a standard language, the non-standard ones spoken by the women folk or the dialects including caste dialects are better and more reliable sources of archaic linguistic elements that are extremely useful in reconstructing the history of a language and its cultural past.

Notes

1. In this paper [T, D, Dh, N, L, S] are used to refer to the voiceless unaspirated retroflex stop, voiced unaspirated retroflex stop, voiced aspirated retroflex stop, retroflex nasal, retroflex lateral, and retroflex sibilant respectively.
2. adabhute subhila: aila: kokua:
dwa:rika: lokaja:ka hoile aca:bhua: (*muSaLi: parba*, p. 11)
'Strangely it was heard, "(The dangerous) Kokua: is coming."
The people of Dwarika became frightened.' (My translation)

References

Anderson, Benedict 1991. *Imagined Communities: Reflections on the Origin and Spread of Nationalism.* London and New York: Verso. (2nd edition, first published in 1983).

Bloomfield, Leonard 1963. *Language.* Delhi: Motilal Banarsidass. (first printed in 1933).

Burrow, Thomas & Murray B. Emeneau 1984. *A Dravidian Etymological Dictionary.* Oxford; Clarendon Press (2nd edition).

Dash, Kulamani (comp.) 1971. *saraLa utkaLa abhidha:na* (A Simple Oriya Dictionary). Cuttack; New Students' Store. (first published in 1932).

Deb, Pramod Chandra 1976. *pramoda abhidha:na* (Pramod Dictionary), Vol. 1 (a-cha). Cuttack: Cuttack Students' Store. (2nd revised edition).

Firth, Raymond 1926. Proverbs in native life with special reference to the Maori. *Folk-Lore XXVII:134-153.*

Lehmann, Winfred P. 1976. *Historical Linguistics: an Introduction.* New Delhi: Oxford & IBH Publishing Co. (first published in 1962).

Mohanty, Panchanan 2002. Two words: two worlds. *Mother Tongue* VII (In Honor of Joseph H. Greenberg), pp. 199-207.

Mohanty, Panchanan 2003. Gender agreement in Oriya: Dravidian or Munda? In: *Agreement in Indian Languages*, ed. by B. Ramakrishna Reddy. Chennai: International Institute of Tamil Studies, pp. 182-192.

Mohanty, Panchanan 2008. Dravidian substratum and Indo-Aryan languages. *International Journal of Dravidian Linguistics*, Volume XXXVII, No. 1, pp. 1-20.

Mohapatra, Dhaneshwar 1976. *oDia: dhwanitattwa o šabda-sambha:ra* (Oriya Phonetics and Vocabulary). Cuttack: Grantha Mandir.

Nanda Sharma, Gopinath (comp.) 2008. *šabdatattwabodha abhidha:na* (An Etymological Dictionary). Cuttack: Friends' Publishers. (first published in 1916).

OBK = oDia: bha:Sa:koSa (The Oriya Language Encyclopedia), Volume 3, 1998; Volume 7, 2005. Cuttack: Arya Prakashan.

Padhi, Baba Baidyanath (comp.) 2008. *br̥hat oDia: abhidha:na* (A Large Oriya Dictionary). Cuttack: Friends' Publishers. (first published in 1964).

Praharaj, Gopal Chandra (comp.) 1931-40. *pu:rNacandra oDia: bhaSa:koSa* (Purnachandra Oriya Language Encyclopedia), Volume I-VII. Cuttack: Utkal Sahitya Press.

sa:raLa: maha:bha:rata (Sarala's Mahabharata) (ed. by Arttaballabha Mohanty) 1965-73. Bhubaneswar: Department of Cultural Affairs, Government of Orissa.

SSN= šri:su:ryara:ya:ndhra nighaNTuvu (Sri Suryaraya Telugu Dictionary). 1998. Hyderabad: Telugu University.

Tripathy, Prafulla Kumar 1987. *samalpuri oDia: šabdakoSa* (Sambalpuri Oriya Dictionary). Bhubaneswar: Orissa Sahitya Academy.

TraduXio: A Collaborative Platform for Multilingual Translation

*Philippe Lacour, Any Freitas, Aurélien Bénel,
Diana Zambon and Franck Eyrau*

Growing international awareness has been raised in the past years about the need to reflect the world's cultural and linguistic diversity at the (public) cyberspace. This concern is all the more sensitive in Asia since economic growth and Internet access have unleashed a desire of mutual cultural recognition. New (technological) challenges arise then from these efforts to 'go multilingual', which have been tackled through more or less efficient translation mechanisms. Yet, for they often rest on a narrow understanding of linguistic pluralism, these mechanisms fall short from addressing the issue in an effective, sustainable and *sensitive* way.

In this paper, we explore an alternative conception of linguistic diversity and propose an alternative way to tackle it. This paper is structured in two parts. In a first moment, we claim that instead of a 'problem' which needs to be 'solved' and/or reduced, linguistic diversity is actually a value that should be cherished and furthered. We claim that contemporary Digital Humanities offer the possibility to harness the power of collaboration to help communities of scholars dedicating themselves to the precise translation of cultural texts. In the second part of this paper, we present an open source Platform which is dedicated specifically to this goal. Traduxio's originality is manifold: it goes beyond the language-pair system, allows for precise suggestions and uses collaborative device. In conclusion, the paper stresses the educational potential of such a virtual electronic environment.

I. e-Linguistic Diversity as a value

Within the last two decades, the preservation and promotion of world's biocultural diversity have gained unprecedented force in the international arena. The awareness that not only ecosystems, but also people, cultures and languages need to be safeguarded and their variety furthered is now recognized as one of the most pressing goals to be achieved through international action. The UNESCO Convention on Cultural Diversity (2005) was in fact one of the first documents to recognize multilingualism as a value to be cherished and promoted at the international level. As an important part of cultural diversity, linguistic diversity was thereby placed as one of the central fields of action of the organization. Acknowledging the specific nature of cultural productions as carriers of "identity, values and meaning", the convention constitutes one of the three pillars of the preservation and promotion of creative diversity[1].

The promotion, protection and preservation of the diversity of languages and cultures have also been embraced as part of the European Union agenda in the field. Member states and European institutions have thus been required to fully embrace these ideas, either by encouraging or assisting citizens in acquiring new language skills[2]. Considering languages as "an integral part of cultural identity"[3], the EU has decided to go a step further and to proclaim 2008 the "European Year of Intercultural Dialogue"[4].

At the same time, technological (r)evolution has been drastically changing communication and other aspects of human relations at the international sphere. The rise of Information and Communication Technologies (ICTs), particularly in the field of education (that is, the so-called ICTE), has brought alternative (more inclusive) forms of producing knowledge, sharing information and acting in world politics. Growing flow of digitized information has been increasing public access to scientific knowledge, education and culture in the last decade, a democratization process that has been particularly felt within humanities and the social sciences (Wikipedia, digital libraries, Open Access Initiative, and so on). Digital technologies have created new methods of learning, teaching, conducting research. All in all, the development of freely accessible, collaborative, intersubjective web-based technologies have launched a kind of 'smooth revolution' in the way scholars and cultural actors produce, reproduce and share knowledge and culture; a 'scientific revolution' that is all the more relevant since it comprises virtually the whole worldwide web.

In this context, notable efforts have been made to promote linguistic diversity in the cyberspace. However, the various attempts to use ITC in order to develop cultural diversity (like Unesco's b@bel initiative, for instance) remain insufficient. Indeed, little informative content is available in the thousands of spoken

---

1 Together with the 1972 Convention concerning the protection of world Cultural and Natural Heritage and the 2003 Convention for the preservation of the Intangible Cultural Heritage. UNESCO has also decided to proclaim 2008 "the International Year of Languages" in order "to promote unity in diversity, global understanding".
2 Calls for the promotion of multilingualism in Europe have become common also within the so-called civil society. The most recent is the 'Plus d'une langue' movement, set up by journalists, academics and intellectuals from different European countries. For details see: www.plus-dune-langue.eu.
3 http://ec.europa.eu/education/languages/index_fr.htm.
4 http://www.interculturaldialogue2008.eu/?L=0.

languages in the world[5]. Neither is there any tool able to create contents in those languages or translate existing information in these idioms.

In fact, one only begins to imagine the possible use of new technologies for the preservation and the concrete development of this cultural wealth, especially as far as international scientific cooperation is concerned. However, digital and cultural cooperation policies worldwide – especially scientific and academic ones – remain too often at the national or supranational levels. This means above all that initiatives and decisions are considerably "top down" (e.g. European framework programs, even when they claim to be "bottom up", are framed in a specific way) and that little room is left open to the creativity of individual users ("grassroot logic"); too often also their capacity to produce content on a collaborative basis is overlooked.

On another level, many organizations, and in particular young associations, are eager to constitute transnational and dynamic networks, based precisely on the principle of sharing and collaborating. If they can benefit from the various but still developing collaborative technologies, these initiatives are soon confronted with the challenge of plurilinguism. This is particularly so for those based or directed to a European public. The assumption that such a difficulty can be solved by the simple elimination of linguistic diversity (often by the adoption of only one, "common" language, namely English) derives from a – well identified though all too frequent – confusion between cultural and communication language.

Though this rather mistaken perception can be understood, the adoption of a common, 'lingua franca', is not really the appropriate answer to linguistic pluralism. On the contrary, instead of insisting in diminishing the plurality, this should be rather promoted, notably by the fostering translation empowered by the use of the new collaborative technologies. Different questions have come up in the last decade regarding the potential use (and value) of these technologies and language/cultural sharing: to what extent these new forms of thinking, communicating and acting can be used to promote world's biocultural diversity?; how can ICTs contribute to the preservation of world's linguistic and cultural complexity instead of reinforcing homogenization?; and, at more specific level, what can ICTs effectively do to reinforce sharing and distribution of knowledge in the media sphere?

In parallel to these reflections, alternative initiatives to improve mutual understanding (and cross cultural fertilization) through language diversity in the cyberspace has been developing. Many of those, though quite novel, have actually proved successful – one can point out here "café babel", or Presseurop, for instance[6]. These initiatives are in fact part of an international trend of media (and cultural) actors which have already started to reflect the importance of language diversity in the

---

5   See http://www.portalingua.info.
6   http://www.cafebabel.com; http://www.presseurop.eu.

cyberspace, mostly by proposing multilingual 'versions' of their content. New (technological and practical) challenges arise then from these efforts to 'go multilingual'. The first one is the growing demand for precise and accurate translation, able to convey the "message" of the text and the "culture" embedded in it. The second challenge is the management of such multilingual content. In fact, once a text is translated, the actual flow of content becomes wider and administrating this diversity can be a major difficulty for media actors if not processed appropriately.

At the time when linguistic diversity becomes greatly recognized as a "value", there is a clear need of a tool to enable actors (single individuals, media organizations, universities, and so forth) to share their concern, approaches, or simply their interested for the same theme. This tool should above all empower these actors and possibly given them a more active role in sharing both information and languages on a transnational basis. As will develop further on, TraduXio aims precisely at addressing some of the challenges.

E. Diversity, Translation, Multilingualism

The recent increase in importance of linguistic diversity as an 'international value' has a direct connection with the expansion of the World Wide Web, which is at the same time the arena in which-, and the medium through which- interactions of all sorts take place. Indeed, the Web allows for the most creative forms of combination of several forms of content, an important part of which (directly or indirectly) linked to a particular form of cultural production. Within this ever evolving, web-based 'cultural production', the (re-)production of language(s) and linguistic practices play a key role.

Translation is one of the most important vectors of multilinguism and E-diversity. Its political potential is huge, ranging from Wikipedia articles for a large public, to classical texts for specialists and researchers. Translation is also at the bottom of processes of dissemination of culture, such as those engendered by immigrants and diasporas worldwide. Its role and application in other fields are countless – and all of crucial importance. In the area of Science and Society, one could consider the role of translation in leveraging multilingual content concerning sustainable development.

In the cultural domain, one could imagine to disseminate works of art though the translation of biographical data. Groups of actors (or artists of different sorts) can moreover be empowered with the capacity to (re)translate classical plays, or create alternative adaptations of existing ones[7]. Finally, and this is the case that

---

7   http://sondes.chartreuse.org/document.php?r=61&id=137.

we shall explore today, one may want to manage multilingual translation content to sustain minority languages on web sites.

Numerous technological efforts have been dedicated to the development and improvement of automatic translation. However, this orientation is still tantamount to considering linguistic diversity as an obstacle to communication, a hindrance to avoid by cutting through semantics as quickly as possible. Though 'rational' and 'pragmatic' at first sight, the idea is comparable to efforts to build a highway in a very hilly landscape: one might not necessarily want to "go faster" and lose all the pleasure of discovering new paths or uncovered aspects of the site while hiking.

Indeed, linguistic diversity can be a pleasure, and a wealth to sustain. And just as much as there is no contradiction between driving your car and talking a walk, there is no exclusive alternative between automatic/fast and precise/slow translation: both are interesting ways to proceed, in their own respective manner, and they should therefore be considered as complementary. Yet, little has been said or effectively done to transform the potential of technologies for precise translation into concrete tools. TraduXio fills in fact this gap, by offering an innovative solution to support collaboration and translation through the web.[8]

The following pages will explore in depth some of the multiple dimensions involved in this enterprise. Starting with some words on the issues at stake concerning media convergence, we will point out the impact of technologically enhanced Linguistic Diversity for the sustainable development of Arts, Culture, Education and Research. The TraduXio project shall then be detailed, in its scientific, technical and legal implications, concluding with concrete considerations.

II. TraduXio

Although some engines have already started to propose functionalities/solutions, we claim that none has gone as far as TraduXio. Employing one of the most original solutions available in the area web-based translation, *TraduXio* presents a number of advantages when compared to existing devices. It is developed by the Zanchin NGO, in collaboration of the University of Technology of Troyes, and with the support of the UNESCO and the International Organization of "Francophonie" (among other partners).

In a nutshell, TraduXio is a free, open source, web based, collaborative, and computer assisted translation tool, developed with innovative technology (a new

---

[8] See Philippe Lacour, Aurélien Bénel, Franck Eyraud, Any Freitas et Diana Zambon, "*TIC, Collaboration et Traduction: vers de nouveaux laboratoires de translocalisation culturelle*", (*ICT, Collaboration and Translation: towards new laboratories of cultural translocalization*), Meta 55(4) Journal for Translators, December 2010.

'Translation Memory' device). Inspired by the strong collaborative spirit of the Web 2.0, and available to different audiences, the software has the vocation to become a mechanism of general interest. Though it has first been experienced in the field of Education, TraduXio has a tremendous potential for other applications: online Media, artistic and educational projects, etc.

TraduXio uses Translation Memory technology in an alternative way. The originality of the software resides in certain of its functionalities – besides the already mentioned ones (freeware, open source, collaborative and designed to cultural texts). Whereas traditional TMs are limited to two languages (the source / the target), *TraduXio* enables the comparison of different versions of the same text. A translated text is in effect not considered as an independent segment, but rather as a version of the initial text in another language.[9]

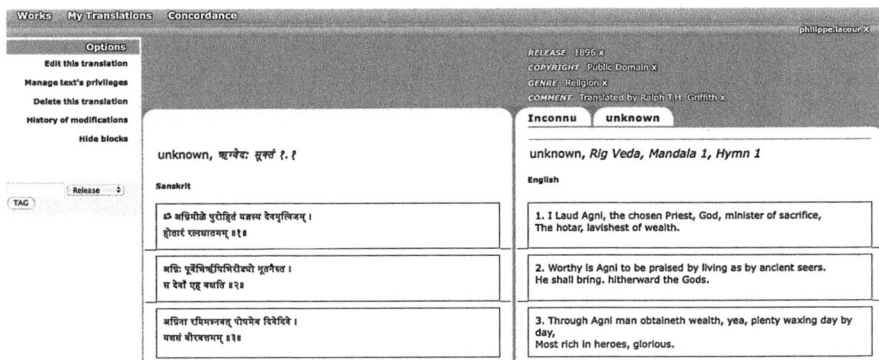

TraduXio offers moreover a better management of the translation context, for it proposes a contextualized classification of the source (i.e. classification of the text according to the history, genre, author, etc.). Thanks to this relevant classification device, information can be more easily assessed and treated, thereby helping users finding the appropriate translation for particular words, expressions, and so forth.

---

9   See Philippe Lacour and Aurélien Bénel, "Towards a Collaborative Platform for Cultural Texts Translators" (with Aurélien Bénel), in Pierre Maret (éd.), *Virtual Community Building and the Information Society: Current and Future Directions*. Hershey (Pennsylvania): **IGI Global**, forthcoming (June 2011).

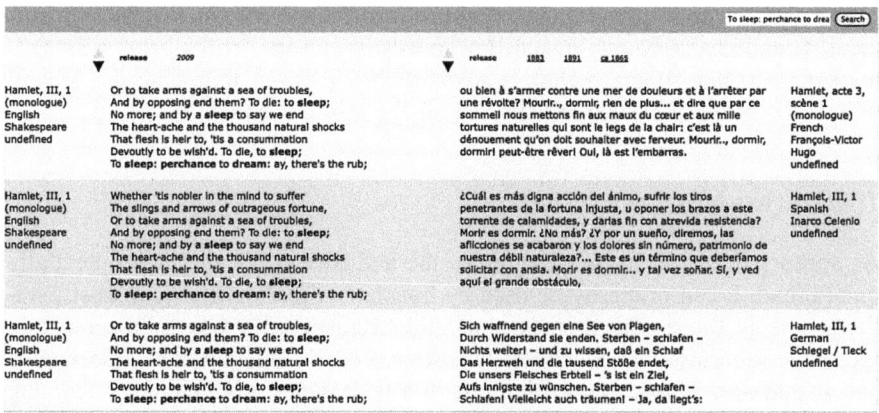

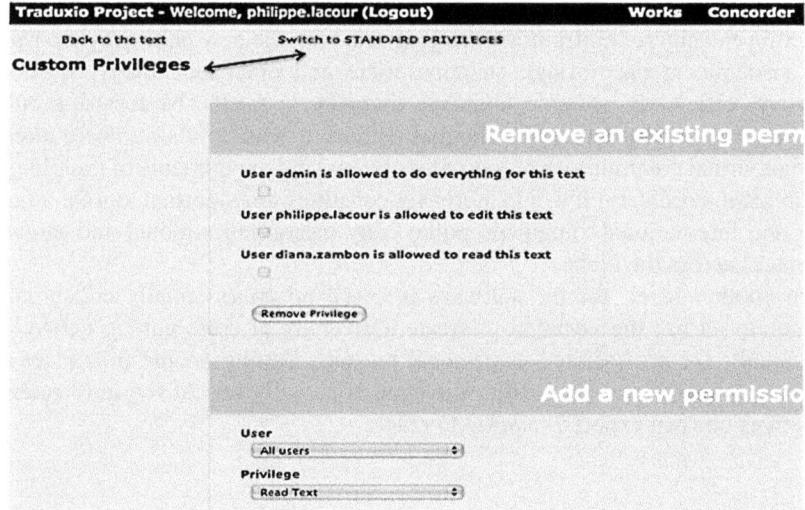

As a collaborative translation software, *TraduXio* is more than a common workbench for digital translators. It is also a network and a platform where translators can meet and create joint projects, exchange ideas, create corpora and glossaries – for the moment, only limited collaborative design have been implemented (revision history, privileges management, etc.). Few platforms, be they commercial (translated.com, proz.com) or non-profit, offer the conjunction of both services. Google has recently launched a Translation Center (still a beta version), a market place that should include a workbench. However, following the general orientation of Google, such initiative should be profit-oriented.[10]

TraduXio to whom?

As appears from the above paragraphs, the audience of *TraduXio* is potentially quite broad. It can primarily be used by translators, researchers, journalists, students and all those who use concepts and language as a way of theoretically reconsidering empirical practices. Likewise, NGOs, international associations and organizations, research institutions in a wide sense, political actors coming across translation problems, professional stage performers re-working previous translations of a theatre play in order to come up with a new version, and so forth are also targeted by the project.

Despite the difficulties of establishing the outcomes of such an enterprise, some of its potential impacts can be sketched out. Firstly, *TraduXio* should help empowering endangered and minority languages at both the new public (cyber-)space and academic arena, through an appropriate and open technology. It should moreover efficiently promote linguistic diversity in media, by fostering online plurilinguism or promoting multilingual edition. It would thus reinforce already existing virtual communities of journalists by making experiments of multilingual mutualization ordinary. It would moreover constitute an important tool for a European and international "linguistic policy", by promoting regional and minority languages across the globe.

On another level, for the software is based on an essentially collaborative technology, it has the vocation to create a diversity of cross cutting network of individuals, for professional or personal reasons. Putting people in contact and fostering inter-cultural (linguistic) dialogue is actually one of the most relevant objectives one can expect *TraduXio* to reach.

Some Legal Considerations

TraduXio is not designed to perform any publishing or editorial functions, but rather to work as a digital workbench and network connecting users/translators worldwide. Translations carried out using TraduXio are thus not intended to be

---

10   See: http://blogoscoped.com/archive/2008-08-04-n48.html.

published or printed by the web-service itself – although authors may personally chose to do so. All content provided by users are integrated to the Translation Memory, which is the foundation and the real differential of the tool. *TraduXio* is hence based on a logic of mutualization in order to create (non financial) value. Its vocation is to become a "commons" (like Creative Commons or Wikimedia Commons) on a non-profit basis. The non-commercial and 'communitarian' dimension of the tool do not imply that the resulting translations will belong to the public domain.

On the contrary, each translator will indeed be given the possibility to tag its creation with a legal license of his choice (e.g. Creative Commons license). The range of rights' attribution goes from the public domain to full copyright. Users will be however encouraged to choose at least an attribution license. Attribution of authority over translations is indeed important since the re-utilization of "memory matching" depends on the identification of the author of a given semantic creation. Frequent users could thus benefit from a form of public and non-financial recognition (a system of "points"), which eventually might turn into a sort of professional reputation. The same liberal approach would apply to databases (the Translation Memory constituted through a specific use of *TraduXio*).[11]

Challenges and solutions

The main challenge in setting up this kind of web-based tool is the establishment (feeding) of an initial database upon which the Translation Memory system can properly run. This particular aspect of the software makes it considerably dependent upon the existence of an important community of users/collaborators from the beginning. Nevertheless, the multiple advantages offered by the software should greatly help persuading potential translators to contribute to the initial feeding of the database, when collaboration is most needed. Another way of addressing this challenge is to rely on strong institutional partners in order to promote the tool and thus gather interest of existing networks and other potential users.

---

11 For more détails, see Philippe Lacour, Any Freitas, Aurélien Bénel, Franck Eyraud et Diana Zambon: « Translation and the New Digital Commons », Tralogy Symposium: « Métiers et technologies de la traduction: quelles convergences pour l'avenir? », Paris, March 3-4 2011, on-line pulication (htt://www.tralogy.eu), retrieved 15.06.2011.

Conclusion

Translators have always played a major role in cultural change in society and in dissemination of knowledge. Not only is translation needed for the construction of national and post-national identity, in India or Europe, for instance, but also for regional and international integration (EU and the Arab/Russian world, India and the other Asian languages). For instance, a lot of vernacular Indian literature has not yet been translated into other Indian languages, not to mention the status of many ancient texts that have not even been transcribed (nor translated) yet.

Though the ICT revolution has launched a new era for digital translation, little has been done to harness linguistic diversity in a sustainable way. Indeed, options such as promoting multilingual translation, using relevant concordance and having people collaborate autonomously have not been systematically explored until now.

TraduXio is a very original CAT tool, designed to encourage the diversification of language learning (in particular the learning of a wider range of languages) and to promote a reappraisal of translation as a professional competence, especially in research activities. Language students can for instance use the platform to propose multilingual translations of assigned texts, either individually or as a group. Language teachers (and/or translation specialists) can easily supervise the translation through the online interface, propose corrections, compare different drafts, and also evaluate students' questions and hesitations.

TraduXio is also suited for scholars and Academic Departments, particularly in Literature and the Social Sciences. Specialists can create multilingual glossaries or build a dedicated 'translation memory' for any topic or author. Users can manage text privileges (who may read, edit, translate, administer …), and thus decide which translations (and to which extent) will be available to the public or remain private.

TraduXio is meant to accommodate linguistic diversity by enforcing multiple translation, thus helping visualize different points of view about a single text, be it within a language (by pointing at the semantic history of a word or an expression) or across various language (different versions of a classical text, like Shakespeare).

Accommodation In Translation:
An Indian Perspective

J. Prabhakara Rao and Jean Peeters

Translation always represents a socially stratified practice. Hence, the strategies involved in it vary from untranslatability on the one end to domestication on the other end. Accommodation as one of the translation strategies lies in between these two ends. The paper deals with diverse aspects of accommodation as a translation procedure. It argues that a careful study of unconsciously developed procedures of accommodation over thousands of years in languages and cultures of Indian sub-continent immensely contribute to translation studies in general and more particularly to the in depth understanding of accommodation in translation.

Translation is recognized as an activity that deals with two different linguistic and cultural systems and operates in two different socio-historical contexts. Hence, the objectives of translating are defined by the needs and expectations of the reader in his culture. As Toury (1985: 18-19) observed "… Translations operate first and foremost in the interest of culture into which they are translating, and not in the interest of source text, let alone the source culture".

One of the interesting and potentially productive areas of research in translation is generally considered to be formulation of means of presentation of source culture in the target language. It is well known fact that in the process of translation there is a need to make compromise between source-text adequacy and target-culture acceptability. Hence, translation and translator act as mediators between source and trarget languages and cultures. The great challenge that a translator normally faces is to make choice between the target text-centred paradigm and the reader-centred paradigm. The reader-centred paradigm is based on all specific translation operations on reader's expectations while the target text-centred paradigm is aimed at creating the perfect target text. These two paradigms are biased towards the target language culture. (Tian Chaunmao, 2009).

Accommodation is increasingly viewed as a major translation procedure especially in cultural translation. The growing emphasis on the analysis of it is, in our view, directly related to the interpretation of dialectical nature of the relationship between language and culture. It is generally stated that language and culture are inseparably linked with each other. The diversity between languages lie, according to German scholar Wilhelm Von Humboldt (1998), not in sounds, words and forms of words only, but in different world-outlook also. The world-outlook is directly expressed in culture by linguistic community. Therefore cultural items can be classified into three types: 1) universal; 2) individual; 3) specific. Universal cultural items (UCIs) present in all languages, hence, translating these items do not pose any problems. Individual cultural items (ICIs) belong to a group of related languages and cultures and consequently such items are easily translatable among that particular group of languages and cultures. Specific cultural items (SCIs) are restricted to source culture, but alien to the target culture (Aixela, 1991). Particularly these items pose problems to the translator. Here, the translator has to really evolve different strategies to accommodate source culture in target language. It indicates that the translator should not only bilingual, but also bicultural.

Accommodation is needed at two levels: linguistic and cultural. It is required only when a particular linguistic or cultural item is absent in the target language. The level of accommodating depends on the diachotomy of relatedness-unrelatedness of languages and cultures. For instance, Nida (1964: 160-161) statement on this issue can be interpreted in terms of accommodation; when the two languages and cultures are genetically related, as in the case of Dravidian, the translator mostly need not have to invoke accommodation procedure; when the languages are unrelated and cultures are related, one need accommodation at linguistic level, for instance, translation among European languages; when the languages are related and cultures are unrelated, the translator makes accommodation for cultural items only; and finally, when both languages and cultures are unrelated, it is obvious that accommodation is required. Basing on such explanation of the link between relatedness-unrelatedness on the one hand and process of accommodation on the other, it may be said that the accommodation process can also be classified into three major types. They include zero accommodation which occurs when the translation takes places between similar languages and cultures; partial accommodation is possible when the relationship is absent either at linguistic level or cultural level; intensive accommodation happens when there is totally no connection between languages and cultures. The relationship between languages, cultures and accommodation is shown in the table-1.

Table-1: Relationship between Languages, Cultures and Accommodation

Languages and Cultures	Linguistic Accommodation	Cultural Accommodation	Type of Accommodation
Related languages and related cultures	−	−	Zero
Unrelated languages and related cultures	+	−	Partial
Related languages and unrelated cultures	−	+	Partial
Unrelated languages and unrelated cultures	+	+	Intensive

+ accommodation required   − accommodation not required

However, the degree of accommodating entirely depends upon the nature of the text. For instance, translation of literary text is an effort at accommodation. Because, it is created in a certain social and cultural contexts in the source language. It is well-recognized fact that the issues involved in translating novels and prose are different from a play. Language in a play text reflect the state of mind, education and personality of the charcters. All these factors pose problems in accommodating linguistic structures in target language.

Another instance could be the translation of philosophic text which create specific problems. Because, any philosophic theory is formulated in a certain historical context. It is not always possible to find the same concepts in target society. Moreover, the creation of any philosophical system has certainly some cultural background also. In such cases, accommodation as a translation procedure fails to be the means of translating. Consequently, translator has to deal with the problem of untranslatability. For instance, translation of Indian philosophical texts into European languages.

Accommodation is sometimes understood in terms of adaptation which is nothing but "the adjustment made to the text" (Burnett: 2010). The adjustment, both at linguistic and cultural level, is made using diverse modes of adaptation. Any culture is not a monolithic entity. It exists in the environment of other cultures and thus being continuously influenced by them. Burnett citing Wolfgang Iser (1994) mentioned that culture "proceeds in mutual appropriation, assimilation, exploitation, interpretation and superimposition". By accepting this statement, it can be concluded that a sort 'unconcious accommodation' is possibly to take place in the society, when cultures are for a long time in a close geographical contact and there is no 'protest' from either side for mutual assimilation. The same is true with languages also. One of central characteristics of Indian society is the assimilation and accommodation of other cultures and languages. Here one should make distinction between 'assimilation' and 'accommodation'. Accommodation, as it was referred earlier, is only just an adjustment where as assimilation means total mingling/acceptance. For instance, the Dravidian and Aryan cultures assimilated by maintaining their distinction. It is interesting to note that despite considerably long presence of Britain, there was not much cultural and linguistic transformation of Indian society. However, it does not mean that the colonial impact is totally absent.

Restructuring is considered by Nida (1982: 163-173) as one of the stages of translation. It basically deals with the styles and varieties of languages. Consequently it can be said that accommodation is not confined to grammar (phonology, morphology, syntax and semantics) and moreover it touches style also. Because, grammar as a cultural figure in translation is always domesticated in target language. So far as style is concerned, the corresponding style may not always available in target language. The issue is further complicated when translator deals with the language with developed literary transition and the language with restricted literary tradition. The existence of diverse regional and social dialects within a language and translation from dialect to another dialect pose different varieties of problems for accommodation. This area is of translation should be properly explored.

The Emeneau's idea 'India as a linguistic area' itself prompts that a great deal of 'linguistic assimilation' and 'linguistic accommodation' has been occurring among different groups of Indian languages over thousands of years. It may be because of this fact it is sometimes difficult to judge whether a particular Sanskrit work in regional languages of India represents a translation or an original creation of the author.

An in-depth study of cultural and linguistic assimilation/ accommodation in Indian sub-continent would undoubtedly provide clues to the translation studies in general. It is not out of place to mention that a remarkable analysis of Indian languages from typological standpoint is currently going on and there is a need to make use of these results for translation and design translation studies procedures and strategies accordingly. Such study provides inputs to the concept 'India as a translation area'.

References

Aixela, JF, 1996. culture-Specific Items in Translation. In R. Alvarez and M.Carmen-Africa Vidal (ed). Translation, Power, Subversion" Philadelphia, P.A, Multilingual Matters Ltd., pp. 52-78.

Burnett, Leon, 2010. Accommodating Brecht: An Indian Endeavour. A paper presented in the International Conference "Socio-Cultural Approaches to Translation: Indian and European Perspectives" 10-12 February, 2010, Hyderabad, India.

Humboldt, Wilhelm Von 1988, The Diversity of Human Language Structure and Its Influence on the Mental Development of Mankind. Translated by Peter Heath with an introduction by Hans Aarselff, Cambridge University Press, Cambridge.

Nida, A. Eugene, 1964. Toward a Science of Translating. Leiden.

Nida, A. Eugene, 1982. The theory and practice of Translation: Leiden.

Toury, Gideon, 1985. A Rationale for Descriptive Translation Studies. In "The Manipulation of Literature" T. Hermans (ed). pp. 16-41.

Tian Chuanmao, 2009. On composite Interrelationship in Literary Translation. A Chinese-English Translation Perspective. Perspectives Studies in Translatology. Vol.16: 384. pp. 143-167.

Multilingual Technical Translation
– A Case of Intercultural Communication

Sumedha Desai

Both "multilingualism" and "intercultural communication" have existed as concepts since ages however these terms are now being discussed heatedly and have come into focus due to the now ubiquitous phenomenon of globalization.

Globalization is understood in many ways but perhaps the most prominent "avtars" of this phenomenon are "economic globalization" and "cultural globalization". "Economic globalization" is understood as economies of various nations interacting with each other and in certain cases even integrating with each other. Cultural globalization has been triggered by transnational migration of people for various reasons, be it for better prospects or for seeking political asylum or other similar reasons. This meeting of cultures and economies has brought multilingualism and intercultural communication at the forefront of discussions in various discourses today. At the same time it has also increased the demand for technical and non-literary translation and that too in multiple languages. This paper will deal with such multilingual translation. The term "technical texts" in the context of this paper encompasses, in addition to technology related texts also other non-literary texts.

Multilingualism and Intercultural Communication

From book reviews and abstracts for congresses and discussions in other fora it is evident that in the present scenario, at the global level, multilingualism is being discussed from various perspectives like the role of nationalism, heritage, culture, identity negotiation, ideology and power in multilingualism (A. Blackage, and A. Creese), its economic and political repercussions, language planning and language policy (P. Nelde) or multilingualism from a sociolinguistic perspective (E.G. Bokamba) to name a few.

The situation of India vis-à-vis multilingualism is interesting. The Indian states are "linguistically" organized on the basis of language identity. At the academic level multilingualism, in India is being discussed in terms of sociology, psychology, pedagogy and demographic aspects of multilingualism (D.P. Pattanayak), multilingualism in India vis-à-vis bilingualism, cultural history of India, minority languages, education (J.C. Sharma, 2001) and other similar topics. At the political and administrative level it is related to language planning and policy.

Multilingualism in India exists not just due to the fact that there are a large number of languages but also because of the social and economic need to be conversant with multiple languages. This need arises due to co-existence of people from different states of India in various cities and towns. Mumbai, the commercial capital of India is a vibrant example of this. From the point of view of translation multilingualism in India is reflected, for example, in the multilingual directives and official notices of the Government agencies of India. These directives and notices are available in at least in three languages viz. English, our link language, Hindi, our national language and the language of the respective state e.g. in Maharashtra it would be in Marathi or in Gujarat it would be in Gujarati.

Intercultural communication, the other field, which came into limelight due to globalization, is also seeing a lot of academic activity. When observing the coming-in-contact of cultures in the new world order one sees a distinct pattern. While the opening up of hitherto controlled economies and increased avenues of trade have brought businesses from the developed nations to the developing and less developed nations the political instability in less developed countries and simply an urge for a better life have sparked transnational migration of people to greener pastures. Both these movements have become a rich source for research in the field of intercultural communication There are innumerable articles on the internet alone describing the various perspectives from which intercultural communication is being studied not to mention the proliferation of books on this topic.

If one surveys the literature on intercultural communication a few topics seem to be dealt with predominantly. In the field of business the topics frequently discussed and highly researched are e.g. the cultural differences in the styles of doing business, business negotiation. Then there are culture-sensitive topics like identity, intercultural misunderstandings, cross cultural awareness, which have received a lot of attention of researchers. Another perspective is the academic perspective, which has seen research work carried out on e.g. theories and models of intercultural communication. It is interesting to note that in most cases, especially in the field of business and also in the socio-cultural area there is a general tone of caution and the emphasis is on, how people of the native culture should avoid cross-cultural communication pitfalls, while communicating with people from other cultures and generally being politically and, if we may say, "culturally" correct.

Multilingual Technical Translation and Intercultural Communication

With regard to the relationship of translation and intercultural communication one can say that translation is a special form of communication and intercultural at that, because it is a means of communication involving two or, in case of multilingual translation, even multiple languages, which in turn are embedded in the different cultures from which these emanate.

The common ground shared by translation and intercultural communication has been explored by translation theorists, prominent among them being Hans Vermeer, who has dealt with translation as intercultural transfer and the translator's intercultural competence especially in his "Skopos theory". In recent times Christina Schäffner (2003) has also enumerated the common assumptions on which translation studies and intercultural communication studies are based. However it is difficult to find research on a linkage between multilingual translation and intercultural communication and my attempts of finding such a link with regard to multilingual technical translation practically drew a blank. Even extensive search in the Internet, since the subject is rather new, did not yield much.

A Google or Yahoo! search for an academic perspective on multilingual technical translation throws up a host of sites dealing mainly with software available for multilingual translation. The topics dealt with here are mostly with reference to machine translation for example multilingual translation of technical service reports by S. Liu et al. (1998) or interactive and evolutionary machine translation technology for multilingual translation (T. Nishigaki 1999), which also deals with non-standard characters like those of the Japanese Kanji script. The internet is teaming with such articles but a direct connection between multilingual technical translation and intercultural communication is not evident.

Although a theoretical framework and even studies linking multilingual technical translation and intercultural communication are not readily available a few examples of multilingual technical translation will be presented here, which will be discussed to highlight the fact that such translations can also be categorized as instances of intercultural communication.

Even though on the one hand it is feared that globalization will create or is creating a sort of a pan global culture and that the identity and variety of cultures and consequently even the languages of these cultures are at a risk of extinction on the other hand there is also a strong endeavour to protect the diversity at the cultural and the linguistic level. The UNESCO Convention on Cultural Diversity (2005) has recognized multilingualism as a value to be cherished and promoted at the international level and that as a part of preserving the cultural diversity efforts are being made to preserve linguistic diversity. In translation this situation has been aptly named by Anthony Pym (2001) as the "diversity paradox" which he explains as follows:

> The diversity paradox may be expressed as an apparent contradiction between, on the one hand, the rise of an international lingua franca, which should lead to lesser linguistic diversity, and on the other, increased use of translation, which should produce greater linguistic diversity.

Various businesses are now providing information regarding their products and services in multiple languages in their attempt to make the most of the opportunity offered by globalization to reach out to customers from different cultures and speaking different languages. Government and public service organizations are now giving information regarding their services in multiple languages in an attempt to reach out to the migrant population in their countries. This is where multilingual translation comes into picture and this is the background of the multilingual translations used as examples in this paper. The aspect of intercultural communication being explored through these examples refers to the content of the text to be translated, which when translated either creates awareness of a cultural concept hitherto scarcely known in the target culture or enhances the semantic dimension of an existing concept in the target culture.

Example from the field of localization

The first example is from the field of localization. This is letter originally written in English and translated in multiple Indian languages as a part of a localization project.

Often multilingual technical translation is associated with software localization. Many translation agencies advertise that they are specialists in multilingual translation and localization. The Localization Industry Standards Association (LISA) defines localization as follows: "Localization involves taking a product and making it linguistically and culturally appropriate to the target locale (country/region and language) where it will be used and sold."[1] However localization is often treated as only a technical problem. Localization experts consider translation as only a small part of localization and that too restricted to "replacement of natural-language strings" (Anthony Pym, 2004). Localization theorists, as Pym (2004) again rightfully says "seem to have made translation into just a language problem".

The letter in this example of localization is addressed by a blog hosting site to the parents of teenagers, who host their own blogs. The gist of this letter is that it

---

1 Definition of localization www.anthealanguages.com/pub/L10n_definitions.pdf.

informs the parents about the migration of these blogs from ABC to XYZ platform. In addition to mentioning the technicalities like the timeline of this migration, the features of the new blog hosting site it also stresses the necessity of the presence of parents when their child migrates from one platform to the other so that they could help the child take decisions, which would be beneficial to the entire family.

This letter is translated in three Indian languages viz. Hindi, Marathi and Gujarati.

First it would be interesting to see some statistics regarding blogging:

If one looks at the statistics of blogging activity on the prominent internet tracking engine Technorati, it shows that in the year 2010 only 12% blogs are from the Asia Pacific region as against e.g. 49% from USA and 29% from the EU. From this one can then imagine the miniscule share of, in the first place Indian blogs, and secondly the microscopic share of the blogs in various Indian languages, which also depicts less awareness of the blogging culture among Indians in general as compared to that of other countries.

When the source, a renowned multilingual translation company, from where this text and its multilingual translation was procured, was contacted to find out the necessity of translating such a letter into the Indian languages one was provided with some interesting information. The answer was that the company, which wanted to get this letter translated into multiple Indian languages envisages that there will be a proliferation of use of software applications like blogs in India in the near future and also that the linguistic diversity in India will be preserved inspite of the onslaught of the global lingua franca and that in the near future such a letter would be required in the various Indian languages.

As regards the linguistic aspects in this example it is observed that all the blog software and technology related words like "migrate", "trackback", "spam" etc. are transliterated in the Indian languages. This could be attributed to the fact that it is difficult to find synonyms for such words in the Indian languages since this technology did not originate in India. More important is the fact that even if such terms are coined in the Indian languages these would hardly be understood. These would in fact sound more foreign than the original English words. The grammatical structure of the letter's translation in Indian languages appears to imitate that of the English structure.

These linguistic features also augment the attempt, even if inadvertent, of creating a sort of pan Indian culture by creating a common vocabulary and grammar, which is not basically from the Indian languages but reaches out to a multitude of people cutting across linguistic borders.

However, coming to intercultural communication angle in this example one pointer to this is the content of the letter, which revolves around blogs, a notion originally from the western culture and hitherto largely unknown to Indian parents intended to read such a translation. This letter is obviously intended to parents, who are most familiar only with their mother tongue, which is one of the Indian vernaculars.

But a more significant aspect of intercultural communication of this letter is the request to parents to assist their teenaged children in taking the decisions. This aspect of parenting is still not predominant in the Indian culture . Even now, in many cases parents "make" the decisions for their children even at the age of 16 or 17 and in matters as significant as the choice of a career. Therefore a call to parents to "assist" their teenaged children in taking decisions is clearly a foreign concept, a concept from the western culture being introduced in the Indian culture. The translation of this letter in multiple Indian languages widens the reach of such a concept to a large group of parents with different linguistic backgrounds.

Example is from the field of health care

Health care being a primary need of every person is a primary service provided by the native country to its migrants. Therefore it is also a vibrant site of intercultural communication, between doctors, patients, care givers, government agencies of the native and the migrant cultures. The domain of health care has seen a lot of research activity from the perspective of intercultural communication as well as multilingual translation.

The example dealt with here is from the domain of health care and is about palliative care, i.e. caring for patients suffering from pain for a long time or patients who are terminally ill. The text here is issued by the Palliative Care Council of South Australia, Palliative Care Victoria and Palliative Care Australia. This text is available in multiple languages. According to the text this palliative care includes a range of services including physical, emotional, social and spiritual and this text is available, among other languages, also in German and Hindi.

In this example too, at the linguistic level there are certain hiccups especially in the Hindi translation like the translation of words like "Chaplain/Religious or Spiritual leader, Bereavement Counsellor" especially in Hindi. The translation of these words into Hindi is difficult because equivalent professions do not exist in the Indian culture. The translation, of these words therefore as "Dharmadhikari" (i.e. one who has the authority to speak about religion)/Dharmik ya Adhyatmik margdarshak" (i.e. religious or spiritual guide) "Viyog ke samay ka salahkar"(a term, which when attempted to be translated into English does not make much sense or its word-for-word translation would be "counselor at the time of separation") sounds out-of-place and can also lead to misunderstandings. Inspite of these hiccups on reading the text one does get an idea that spiritual help is also available in palliative care.

An interesting aspect in this particular example linguistically is that in comparison to the Hindi translation the German translation is much smoother. The abovementioned terms do not sound odd when translated in the German language e.g. "Bereavement counselor" is translated as "Trauerberater", which is now also a profession, for which one can train. This "smoothness" of translation could be attributed to the fact that both the languages emanate from similar cultures.

Nevertheless from this example too one can gain insights from the perspective of intercultural communication especially between the English-speaking Australian communities and the Hindi-speaking people of Indian origin.

Actually the concept of palliative care is not a widely known concept in India. One does not find many such institutions in India. A terminally ill person is generally at home either looked after by the family members and if the family can afford, then by care-givers. A doctor is called in as and when required. However a religious or spiritual leader is not called at home and the concept of a bereavement counselor is almost non-existent. In fact in our ancient scripture there is a treatise written by a well known doctor of that time by the name Charak', which in addition to the information on medicinal plants and medicine also consists of several other aspects related to medicine. At one place in this treatise the author describes the duties of an Ayurvedic doctor, which include the duty of preparing a terminally patient to face death and to prepare the family of the patient to bear the loss of the family member. Therefore this institutionalized form of care for terminally ill people is a new concept for primarily Hindi speaking Indians, for whom such a text is intended. Therefore the translation of this text into Hindi has introduced a new cultural concept in the consciousness of the "Hindi reading" person. It has made him aware of availability of even spiritual help in the institutionalized format of medical care!

Example from the field of Public Service

The third example is related to the introduction of a new understanding of a familiar institution namely "public library".

This text is from the public library of a well-known city in Canada. This is available, in addition to many other languages, even in English and Gujarati, an Indian language. This text talks about the benefits of joining the public library, which are apparently meant for immigrants to Canada. These benefits are that by joining the public library one can help one's child succeed in school, learn about services for newcomers, get information about finding a job, have fun with the family in addition to borrowing books and CDs and videos in many languages.

The public library to a person from India, in this example the Gujarati speaking people, is mainly a place where one can borrow and read books and other printed and audio-visual material. Not much different from a regular library of an institution, though some public libraries do have projects for conserving rare books and other printed material. However that the public library provides assistance to help one's child succeed in school, people can learn about services for newcomers, get information about finding a job, have fun with the family in addition to borrowing books, CD's and videos in multiple languages is a new concept introduced to the Gujarati speaking people.

All these examples have tried to focus on the intercultural communication evident even in technical and non-literary multilingual translations.

Conclusion

Today in the literature on intercultural communication it is often emphasized that in order to have smooth intercultural communication and facilitate "integration" of people from other cultures the native culture has to show understanding towards the people coming from other countries and cultures. However these examples indicate that there is much intercultural learning for the people from the foreign cultures from such translation. Such translation not only provides factual information, which is no-doubt its primary function, but also communicates cultural concepts, with which the recipients of such translations are not familiar.

These examples are no doubt a source for studying translation from the popular perspectives like its linguistic aspects, the notion of equivalence, text typology and others. However this paper has been an attempt to go beyond these perspectives and see technical and non-literary translation from a different perspective. These examples show how in addition to providing information the technical and non-literary translation of texts are also instances of intercultural communication.

This paper attempts to view intercultural communication between people of different cultures on the backdrop of translation of the technical and non-literary discourse. With the help of examples from diverse fields it has been attempted to highlight the role of multilingual technical translation in fostering the understanding of concepts rooted in one culture by people from another culture, where perhaps such concepts are not the norm or are non-existent. Thus such multilingual technical translations become sites of intercultural communication.

References

Blackage, A. and Creese, A, "Multilingualism A Critical Perspective", www.continuumbooks.com/books/detail.aspx?BookId=125623&.

Bokamba, E.G. "Multilingualism as a Sociolinguistic Phenomenon: an African Perspective", http://www.inst.at/kctos/speakers_a-f/bokamba.htm.

Liu, S. Hui, S.C. Foo, S. and Leong, P.C. 1998, "Online Multilingual Translation of Technical Service Reports over the World Wide Web", http://www.journal.au.edu/ijcim/august98/online_2.html.

Nelde, P. "New Multilingualism-Perspectives For A European Language Policy – economic and political repercussions of multilingualism in the European Union", http://www.fernuni-hagen.de/sprachen/kongress/Abstracts/Nelde EN.pdf.

Nishigaki, T. 1999, "What Can MT Do for Multilingualism on the Net?", www.mt-archive.info/MTS-1999-Nishigaki.pdf.

Pattanayak, D.P. (ed.), "Multilingualism in India", http://www.vedamsbooks.in/no47719/multilingualism-india-edited-by-debi-prasanna-pattanayak.

Pym, A. 2001, "Translation and International Institutions. Explaining the Diversity Paradox", http://www.tinet.cat/~apym/on-line/translation/diversity.html.

Pym, A. 2004, "Localization from the Perspective of Translation Studies: Overlaps in the Digital Divide?", http://www.elda.org/en/proj/scalla/SCALLA 2004/Pymv2.pdf.

Schäffner, C. 2003, "Translation and Intercultural communication: Similarities and differences", *Studies in Communication Sciences* 3/2 79-107.

Sharma, J.C.2001, " Multilingualism in India", http://www.languageinindia.com/dec2001/jcsharma2.html.

Source of example texts

Localization: Lionbridge Technologies Pvt. Ltd., Mumbai
Health care:
http://www.mhcs.health.nsw.gov.au/publication_pdfs/7955/AHS-7955-HIN.pdf.
http://www.mhcs.health.nsw.gov.au/publication_pdfs/7955/AHS-7955-ENG.pdf.
http://www.mhcs.health.nsw.gov.au/publication_pdfs/7955/AHS-7955-GER.pdf.

Public Service:

http://www.settlement.org/downloads/SWIS_Library_English.pdf.
http://www.settlement.org/downloads/SWIS_Library_Gujarati.pdf.

Translating Woman:
Feminist Translation in Nicole Brossard

Sushma V. Murthy

Debates around language – both discourses on language and the language of discourse have been central to feminist theory and practice. Post-modern feminist theories locate woman's subjectivity or the 'lack of it' by exploring the relationship between language and reality and establishing these domains as inherently masculine. Women's relationship with language, therefore, has always been defined as absence or one of the 'outsider'. In effect, feminisms across the world have not only largely defined the female/feminine in relation to the male/masculine, but significantly so as 'lack' or 'difference' in relation to the semiotic. Feminism's pre-occupation with the phal(logo)centric symbolic order is paradoxically both the beginning and end of feminist discourse.

For instance, in "Extracts from Man Made Language", Dale Spender, terms language as "… both a creative and an inhibiting vehicle … we resist, fear and dread any modifications to the structures we have initially created, a language trap." (Spender, 1998, 93-100)

What Dale Spender describes as an act of resistance is often transcended in feminist theory by a strong advocacy for women's writing. However, the quest for women's subjectivities in writing is entrenched in the notion that women's language is essentially 'different' from, therefore (repeatedly and unconsciously) placed in relation to men. Kristeva's point, for example, that women don't have a proper place within the symbolic or Dale Spender's statement that women cannot "fit into" language that is "essentially man-made" (Spender, 1998, 93-100) questions the ideological while at the same time divests women of their subjective positions that are neither 'within' nor 'without' the symbolic 'order'.

The link between language and identity that is crucial to feminist politics is often weakened by close linguistic analysis that essentially grounds language to the realm of apparatus: a set of devices, man-made, fixed, pre-conditioned by among other constructs, sentence structure and the act of fixing meaning through the process of naming.

The objective of this paper is to deconstruct popular feminist understandings of language as system and establish feminist translation as a radical attempt at perceiving language as discourse, vis a vis the work of Quebecoise lesbian feminist writer, Nicole Brossard. The paper will attempt to debate that feminist translation by virtue of being a feminist act is not just women translating women, but the act of women *writing* women. Writing and Translation, in being literally and figuratively constructed that way, are commonly perceived as translation following writing, creating a space that is alike, in a different language. Feminist translations of Nicole Brossard not only derive from her writing, but feed into it. Translation becomes not an act of departure from the 'original', but an arrival at shared feminist understanding.

Nicole Brossard is one of the most prominent avant-garde writers of Canada who emerged as a writer from the volatile nationalist movement of modernity in the 1960s, during the aftermath of Quebec's Quiet Revolution. In the thick of motherhood, Brossard came out as lesbian, and that meant to her, writing not just her body, but a body in relation to women's bodies. Her constant reiteration of the need for a lesbian to "literally" (Brossard, 1988) give birth to herself or risk the reality of becoming fiction forever, underlines her preoccupation with translation. Brossard believes that the act of em/bodying oneself in language as a lesbian is also an act of bodying forth. Hence, her writing on the one hand articulates the desire for 'woman' (very different from the classical feminist notion of women), and her translations on the other take the desiring body forth, into a collective attempt at reiterating woman.

Feminist translation as a re/it/eration and re/in/scribing of identities is a subversive act that appropriates the classical patriarchal device of constant invocation to fix meanings. Language as a radical process of creating meanings as against a set of codes arranged to hold a mirror to so-called reality is central to most feminist discourses. Feminist practices around language have sought to trace how and why ideologies have been time and again constructed in language in terms of gender identification through sexual difference. The seemingly perpetual enactment of identities through ideologies, constantly understood by feminist linguists as naming, an attempt to re-establish rules already in place, is a continuous process of fixing meanings through re/presentation. Ideologies worldwide, including sexist discourses, are legitimized by re/presentation. What in other words is simply understood as 'common knowledge' is a set of ideologies made legitimate by covert processes where meanings become naturalized and normalized. Translation by virtue of its innate quality of be/coming, not be/ing ,is language in process, language that constantly eludes meaning and shifts from fixed understandings to discursive methods of making new meanings. Imbued with such multiplicity, translation, in lesbian feminist contexts, such as those of Brossard, lends itself to the dynamics of recreation of meanings, thereby re/presenting, to break the imperatives of re/presentation. Feminist translations push language beyond established realms of meaning, beyond sheer precipices that loom large and make crossing-overs into the inarticulate world, slippery and frightening. They shatter con/structs and widen the frontiers of language to accommodate processes of construction.

Nicole Brossard is not only one of the most widely translated lesbian writers; her translations into English have opened up dynamic spaces for feminist translation theory. Translation is a conscious feminist act in Brossard, a creation of women's space in writing that makes living in a woman's skin, speaking from a woman's tongue, an experience accessible to varied linguistic and cultural understandings. One of Brossard's collection of poems titled *French Kiss* describes perfectly the free libidinal space, the melting of meanings that characterizes the 'Ecriture Feminine' of her translations. The process of translation becomes the act of touching a woman's body, a sliding of meaning, a tasting of the grain of one's experience as woman on another woman's tongue. The process of writing, therefore, becomes the act of translating oneself as a woman and the act of translating, a process of writing oneself. To this effect, writing and translation are inextricably rendered into *one process*.

Beginning with the idea that there can be no 'actual' experience in writing, and that writing is only a translation of experience, all writing amounts to translation. One set of linguistic tools (available to the author at the time of translating the 'actual', in effect, recalled experience) constitutes writing at a given point of time. Given the fact that so many or only as many linguistic tools were available to the 'author' at a given point of time, writing is never 'original' or 'complete'. In 'Le Desert Mauve', Nicole Brossard captures the fluidity of language by self-translating the first part of the book, symbolically, and interestingly into the same language in the third part and subverts conventional notions of translation, thereby displacing non-linear understandings of identity and experience. Furthermore, the two parts are interspersed by a series of pictures, a visual re/presentation of the character Longman who features in both versions of print on either side. Meanings literally get displaced on either side of 'real/ity' in this work which translates itself. Brossard captures the fluid nuances of the lesbian body in the arbitrariness of language that constantly deludes itself, and has to be made sense of by a constant revoking of meanings through translation. *Le Mauve Desert*, later translated into *Mauve Desert,* renewed the cyclical process of writing as translation in a certain seamless rendering of translation into what Susanne de Lotbiniere – Harwood, the translator, terms as a "re-writing in the feminine" (Harwood, 1991). *Mauve Desert* in essence becomes a feminist work that evokes the power of translation to re/create meanings for women in four different texts which, to borrow an ideology from Erin Moure, "transelate" (Moure, 2001) one another in the new found(ed) joy of lesbian identities.

Brossard's *Baroque de L'aube*, translated with the title, *Baroque at Dawn* finds Brossard donning her own character in the novel, living the character, bodying herself forth within the pages, uttering the guttural idea of the text as a process of voicing oneself, writing oneself, translating oneself in virtual reality, for in Brossard's own words,

> "Reality is what we invent"
>
> and
>
> "Woman's reality is a fiction"
> (Brossard, 1988)

English translators of Brossard's feminist works in French have sought to de/rivet sexist underpinnings of the language while at the same time drawing attention to what is normally assumed to be the more sexist of the two languages, namely French. Susanne Harwood, for instance creates the word 'auther' to underline the fact that she is translating a woman from the subjective position of a woman and the term "He-man language" to describe English which she believes is just as sexist as French, not very obviously, but covertly so, in its hidden constructions. Brossard herself appropriates a curious intermingling of English and French to create her idea of "the integral woman", namely the "essentielle woman" (not in the essentialist sense of woman). The binary opposition of source and translation is effectively crippled through such discursive acts where women translate each other to inscribe each other's subjectivities. And translation effectually occurs in little acts of identification rather than in the workings of a different language, for the language of feminist translation is the same in spite of identity politics and varied subjective positions – the language of women.

Works Cited

Brossard, Nicole. 1988, *The Aerial Letter*. Translated by Marlene Wildeman. Toronto: The Women's Press.
–. 1987, *Le Desert Mauve*. Quebec: Editions de l'Hexagone.
–. 1990, *Mauve Desert*. Translated by Susanne de Lotbiniere-Harwood. Toronto: The Coach House Press.
–. 1995, *Baroque de L'aube*. Quebec: Editions de l'Hexagone.
–. 1997, *Baroque at Dawn*. Toronto: McClelland & Stewart.Inc.
–. 1986, *French Kiss, or, A Pang's progress*. Toronto: Coach House Press.
de Lotbiniere-Harwood, Susanne. 1991, *The Body Bilingual: Translation as a Re-writing in the Feminine*. Toronto: The Women's Press.

Kristeva, Julia. 1980, "Woman can never be defined". In New French Feminisms, edited by Elaine Marks and Isabelle Courtivron, 137-8. New York: Shocken Books

Moure, Erin. 2001, Sheep's vigil by a fervent person: A translation of Alberto Caeiro/ Fernando Pessoa's Oguardador de rebanhos. Toronto: House of Anansi Press.

Spender, Dale. 1998. "Extracts from Man-made Language". In The Feminist Critique of Language: A Reader, edited by Deborah Cameron., 93-100. London and New York: Routledge. Originally published in Dale Spender. *Man Made Language* (London: Routledge & Kegan Paul. Ltd., 1980).

www.ingramcontent.com/pod-product-compliance
Ingram Content Group UK Ltd.
Pitfield, Milton Keynes, MK11 3LW, UK
UKHW021836210426
5322IPUK00021B/316